Customer-Centricity in Organized Retailing

Manoj Kumar Dash · Manash Kumar Sahu ·
Jishnu Bhattacharyya · Shivam Sakshi

Customer-Centricity in Organized Retailing

A Guide to the Basis of Winning Strategies

Manoj Kumar Dash
ABV-Indian Institute of Information Technology and Management
Gwalior, Madhya Pradesh, India

Jishnu Bhattacharyya
University of Nottingham Ningbo China
Ningbo, China

Manash Kumar Sahu
ASBM University
Bhubaneswar, Odisha, India

Shivam Sakshi
VIT Business School, Vellore Institute of Technology
Vellore, Tamil Nadu, India

ISBN 978-981-19-3592-3   ISBN 978-981-19-3593-0 (eBook)
https://doi.org/10.1007/978-981-19-3593-0

© The Editor(s) (if applicable) and The Author(s), under exclusive license to Springer Nature Singapore Pte Ltd. 2023

This work is subject to copyright. All rights are solely and exclusively licensed by the Publisher, whether the whole or part of the material is concerned, specifically the rights of translation, reprinting, reuse of illustrations, recitation, broadcasting, reproduction on microfilms or in any other physical way, and transmission or information storage and retrieval, electronic adaptation, computer software, or by similar or dissimilar methodology now known or hereafter developed.

The use of general descriptive names, registered names, trademarks, service marks, etc. in this publication does not imply, even in the absence of a specific statement, that such names are exempt from the relevant protective laws and regulations and therefore free for general use.

The publisher, the authors, and the editors are safe to assume that the advice and information in this book are believed to be true and accurate at the date of publication. Neither the publisher nor the authors or the editors give a warranty, expressed or implied, with respect to the material contained herein or for any errors or omissions that may have been made. The publisher remains neutral with regard to jurisdictional claims in published maps and institutional affiliations.

This Palgrave Macmillan imprint is published by the registered company Springer Nature Singapore Pte Ltd.
The registered company address is: 152 Beach Road, #21-01/04 Gateway East, Singapore 189721, Singapore

"We dedicate this book to our family, who supported and encouraged us in our journey."

—*Authors*

About This Book

Customer-centric organized retailing is a fascinating field of study within marketing. Currently, organized retailers make up a small portion of the fragmented retail landscape. Consumers are gradually gravitating toward organized retail due to demographic and socioeconomic changes and a desire for an improved shopping experience. In addressing customer needs and developing successful retailing strategies, organized retailing in emerging economies with changing consumer behavior is an exciting yet complex task for businesses. The retail industry is currently being buffeted by increased competition, particularly from new retailing formats and the entry of new players. As a result, developing appropriate retailing strategies in the context of an emerging economy makes sense for retail practitioners. Retailers must be agile and forward-thinking to implement a customer-centric approach across the retail value chain's upstream and downstream actions. Retailers in emerging markets, in particular, require clarity on the exact tools and techniques that will allow them to move from their present product-centric state to the looked-for customer-centric state. This book is a compendium of cutting-edge knowledge for an effective retailing strategy, with crisp and insightful lessons from India.

This book is dedicated to assisting practitioners in developing and implementing a customer-centric culture in practice, and it focuses on various retail strategy concepts and their implementation in practice. It intends to present the multifaceted and diverse retail marketing issues in the form of two studies, each of which provides a comprehensive solution in practice. The book demonstrates how to apply Structural Equation Modeling and the Analytic Hierarchy Process in developing retailing strategy.

Contents

Part I Introduction: Theory, Concepts, and Strategy

1 Introduction: Customer-Centric Retailing in Emerging
  Markets   3
  Chapters in This Book   5
  References   7

2 Customer-Centricity: The Quest for Customer Focus   9
  Introduction   9
  Conclusion   21
  References   22

3 Organized Retailing: A Brief Introduction   25
  Introduction   25
  What is Organized Retailing?   26
  Organized Retailing in Emerging Markets   27
  Challenges in Organized Retailing in Emerging Markets   30
  Customer-centricity in Organized Retailing   31
  Ways to Increase Customer-centricity in Retailing   32
  Conclusion   33
  References   34

ix

Part II Empirical Studies—Concepts and Implementations

4 Customer Segmentation: SMPI Model — 39
Introduction — 39
Segmentation of Organized Retail Store Shoppers — 41
Pillars of Customer-Centricity — 45
Empirical Analysis — 52
Moderating Effects of Consumer Demographics on the SMPI Model — 81
The Implication of Research Work — 84
Conclusion — 85
References — 86

5 Strategic Mismatch: IAHP — 91
Introduction — 91
Consumer Decision-Making Models — 93
The Prescribed Solutions — 95
Complex Decision-Making and MCDM — 97
Consumer Shopping Behavior and Preferences — 97
Research Methodology — 100
The Analytical Hierarchy Process Methodology — 104
Formulation of AHP — 104
Research Design and Methodology — 111
Empirical Analysis — 127
Analysis of Local and Global Weight of Consumer Preferences (Consumer Perspective) — 135
Analysis of Local and Global Weight of Retailers' Counter-Strategies (Retailer Perspective) — 150
Implications of Results (AHP for Consumers' Perspective vs. iAHP for Retailers' Perspective) — 157
Conclusion — 162
References — 163

Recommended Readings — 171
Index — 173

About the Authors

Manoj Kumar Dash has been researching actively with regular journal and book publications. A few of his recent publications are journals like the *International Journal of Production Research, Online Information Review, International Journal of Emerging Markets, IJIM Data Insights, Benchmarking: An International Journal, Telemetric and Informatics, Neural Computing and Application*, etc. He has to his credit several best paper awards like the Best Research paper Award in Marketing in International Conference of Arts and Science organized by Harvard University (USA) Boston. Besides being associate professor at the Indian Institute of Information Technology and Management Gwalior, he is also a visiting faculty in IIM Indore. He has also served as Adjunct faculty at Lancaster University UK and visiting professor at SIOM Nashik. He had conducted several Faculty Development Programs on Multivariate Analysis, Econometrics, Research Methodology, Multi-Criteria Optimization, Multivariate analysis in Marketing, etc. He delivered lectures as a resource person and keynote speaker in multiple programs organized by reputed institutes in India. He is specialized in Marketing Analytics. He was involved as Chair Member in International Conference at Harvard University, USA. He has supervised several Ph.Ds. who are serving in academic positions across the globe.

Manash Kumar Sahu is currently working as an assistant professor in marketing at ASBM University in Bhubaneshwar, Odisha. His educational qualifications include a Ph.D. degree from Berhampur University, a Master of Business Administration degree from Berhampur University, and a Bachelor of Arts from Sambalpur University, Odisha. His research areas include a wide variety of approaches toward customers and marketing platforms like Customer-Centricity, Consumer Behavior (Retail), Customer Relationship Management(CRM), and Digital & Social Media Marketing (DSM). His Doctoral dissertation topic was on Customer-Centric Business Modeling (CCBM) in Organized Retailing concerning Consumer Shopping Behavior and Preferences. Over the years, he has authored many academic articles and has papers in the pipeline for some leading academic journals. He was awarded the Research Scholar Award for "Outstanding Research Publications" in the Professional Stream of Berhampur University for 2014 (Best Research Scholar Award). Apart from publications, he has also participated in an impressive number of faculty development programs and academic development programs.

Dr. Sahu has been in various teaching positions dealing with undergraduate and post-graduate students over the years. He serves as an assistant editor for ASBM Journal of Management, besides being a Research and Development Cell coordinator at ASBM University, Bhubaneswar, Odisha. He is also a student affairs Chair-Person at the Asian School of Business Management (ASBM), Bhubaneswar, Odisha.

Jishnu Bhattacharyya is a Ph.D. candidate in marketing at the University of Nottingham. In academia, he has worked as a Project Scientist for the Indian Institute of Technology Delhi. He enjoys asking questions that are both practically motivated and theoretically inspired along several interconnected research streams, including but not limited to sustainability communication, socially responsible consumption, consumer interactions with technology, and services marketing. He has received awards for his academic and research excellence. His research has appeared in the Journal of Business Research.

Shivam Sakshi is an Assistant Professor at VIT Business School, Vellore Institute of Technology, Vellore, Tamil Nadu, India. He was a Postdoctoral Associate at the Indian Institute of Management Bangalore.

Shivam holds a Ph.D. in Economics and Business from the University of Debrecen, Hungary, and an M.B.A. from the Indian Institute of Information Technology and Management Gwalior. He was an awardee of a full scholarship for his doctoral studies. Before enrolling in the Ph.D. program, he worked at the National Institute of Rural Development and Panchayati Raj, Hyderabad, as Senior Project Training Manager for a project under the Ministry of Rural Development and Panchayati Raj Government India. Shivam's academic research encompasses a broad spectrum of research areas such as customer-centricity, consumer behavior, consumer decision-making styles, online marketing, rural markets, etc.

While doing his Ph.D., he has involved in extensive teaching at the University of Debrecen. Since 2017, he has been involved in teaching various subjects related to economics and business to M.Sc. and B.Sc. students at his department. In his career, Shivam has always been a passionate individual with a keen interest in spreading knowledge, and he has chosen teaching as the medium of actualizing his interest.

LIST OF FIGURES

Fig. 4.1　Confirmatory factor structure of consumers' preferred attributes in organized retailing (*NB* SA—Store Atmospherics, P.V.—Pricing and Value, AST—Assortment, ISD—In-store Delights, CNV—Convenience, PSQR—Product/Service Quality and Reliability, PPE—Person-to-Person Experience, P.S.—Problem-Solving, ENT—Entertainment. *Source* Developed by authors in AMOS 20.0 using Primary Data)　73

Fig. 4.2　Confirmatory factor structure of consumer shopping motivation and patronage intention in organized retailing (*Source* Developed by authors in AMOS 20.0 using Primary Data. This figure depicts the constructs of consumers' shopping motivation and patronage intention in organized retailing)　74

Fig. 4.3　Hypothetical structural model of pillars of customer-centricity: *Preference-Motivation-Patronage (PMP Model)* (*Source* Developed by authors)　75

Fig. 4.4　Structural model shopping motivation and patronage intention (SMPI Model) in organized retailing (*Source* Developed by authors in AMOS 20.0 using Primary Data. This figure depicts the structural model of pillars of customer-centricity in organized retailing)　76

Fig. 4.5	Result of hypotheses testing (*Source* Estimated from Primary Data) (*Significant at 0.05 [$p < 0.05$], **Significant at 0.01 [$p < 0.01$], ***Significant at 0.001 [$p < 0.001$])	80
Fig. 4.6	Moderating effect of consumers' demographics on SMPI model (*Source* Developed by authors in AMOS 20.0 with Insights from Primary Data Analysis)	82
Fig. 5.1	AHP-based calculation and prioritization flow diagram	101
Fig. 5.2	Goal, criteria, and sub-criteria of consumer preference hierarchy (*Source* Developed by authors)	121
Fig. 5.3	Goal, criteria, and sub-criteria of retailers' strategy hierarchy (*Source* Developed by authors)	122
Fig. 5.4	Visualization of local and global weights of consumer preference	148
Fig. 5.5	Visualization of local and global weights of retailers' counter strategy & sub-strategies (*Source* Estimated from Primary Data)	156

List of Tables

Table 3.1	Difference between organized and unorganized retail sectors	28
Table 4.1	Research procedure followed	47
Table 4.2	Identified consumers' preferred attributes/factors in organized retailing	54
Table 4.3	Re-identified constructs for consumers' shopping motivation and patronage intention in organized retailing	60
Table 4.4	Reliability of identified factors for consumer preference scale	64
Table 4.5	Discriminant validity of consumer preference scale (AVE and squared inter-construct correlations—SIC Comparison)	67
Table 4.6	Reliability of re-identified factor structure for consumer shopping motivation and patronage intention	68
Table 4.7	Goodness-of-fit results of shopping motivation and patronage intention measurement model	70
Table 4.8	Discriminant validity for shopping motivation and patronage intention (AVE and squared interconstruct correlations—SIC comparison)	70
Table 4.9	Path estimates for SMPI model of customer-centricity	71
Table 4.10	Goodness-of-fit of structural model of customer-centricity: PMP model of moderating effects	77
Table 4.11	Summarized result of segmentation of organized retail store shoppers based on moderating effect of consumer demographics on SMPI model of customer-centricity	78

xvii

Table 5.1	Research process	99
Table 5.2	The semantic scale for AHP	103
Table 5.3	The random consistency index (RI) for different matrix sizes	106
Table 5.4	Factors and sub-factors of consumer preferences in organized retailing	108
Table 5.5	Definitions of the dimension and judgments used in the study (consumer perspective)	110
Table 5.6	Interpreted strategy and sub-strategies vis-à-vis consumers' preferred factors and sub-factors	112
Table 5.7	Definitions of the dimension and judgments used in the study (retailer perspective)	114
Table 5.8	Evaluators' profile (Group 1: heavy and loyal customers)	125
Table 5.9	Experts' profile (Group 2: Academic & retail industry experts)	126
Table 5.10	Steps for estimation procedure of AHP, iAHP and consistency check	136
Table 5.11	Calculation of normalized matrix for AHP (Consumer Perspective)	137
Table 5.12	Calculation of Weighted Vector (WV) Matrix (Consumer Perspective)	138
Table 5.13	Calculation of eigen value (consumer perspective)	139
Table 5.14	Priority ranks of consumers' preferred factors	140
Table 5.15	Local and global weights of consumer preference factors and sub-factors	141
Table 5.16	Top and bottom five sub-factors of consumer preference	149
Table 5.17	Local and global weights of retailers' counter-strategy and sub-strategies	151
Table 5.18	Top and bottom five sub-strategies of retailers' priority	157
Table 5.19	The priority matrix: consumer vs. retailer perspective in organized retailing context	158
Table 5.20	Comparative analysis of consumers' vs. retailers' priorities (sub-criteria wise)	161

PART I

Introduction: Theory, Concepts, and Strategy

CHAPTER 1

Introduction: Customer-Centric Retailing in Emerging Markets

Customer-centricity, or putting your customer at the center of your strategy, has long been regarded as the "holy grail of retail marketing" (Latinovic & Chatterjee, 2019). Customer-centricity and its benefits have been debated for over 60 years (Shah et al., 2006). Throughout history, scholars in marketing (e.g., Lee et al., 2015; Sheth et al., 2000), as well as other areas such as information systems (e.g., Wagner & Majchrzak, 2006), hospitality (e.g., Inversini et al., 2020), and innovation management (e.g., Selden & MacMillan, 2006), have referred to customer-centricity as an incumbent challenge for businesses. Customer-centricity is a buzzword in public social mentions (Mentions: 610, Users: 328, Sentiment: 9:1; 21 October 2021 at 00:18 a.m. IST) (Social Searcher, 2021). Companies like Wegmans, Trader Joe's, and Glossier have prioritized customer-centricity in their pursuit of competitive advantage and are among the top 100 most customer-centric companies in the world (Morgan, 2019). However, most of these companies are from developed markets that have adopted a customer-centric approach in response to global competition. As evidenced by academic literature and practice, this is a burgeoning research area that aims to capture current developments in the business world, predict future developments, and make sense of the concept and its elements.

© The Author(s), under exclusive license to Springer Nature Singapore Pte Ltd. 2023
M. K. Dash et al., *Customer-Centricity in Organized Retailing*,
https://doi.org/10.1007/978-981-19-3593-0_1

Despite this emphasis, many businesses continue to struggle to align with the customer-centric paradigm fully. Customer-centricity has remained one of the most contentious marketing concepts (Gummesson, 2008) and is often regarded as a highly fluid and ambiguous subject (Lamberti, 2013). According to prior studies, despite the relevant attention devoted by both scholars and practitioners, our understanding of how to implement customer-centricity is considerably limited (e.g., Lamberti, 2013). In particular, retailers in emerging markets (EMs) necessitate clarity on developing strategies that will allow them to attain the desired customer-centric state (Gupta & Ramachandran, 2021). The study of EMs is worthwhile because they account for around 86 percent of the world's population as of 2020 (OECD, 2018), and retail sales in EMs (e.g., India, China) is expected to grow at a rate of 4.4 percent per year to reach more than $17.8 trillion in 2030, up from $9.2 trillion in 2015 (Ben-Shabat et al., 2016). The EMs contrast considerably from developed markets on numerous dimensions, such as "market heterogeneity, socio-political governance, chronic resource shortage, and inadequate infrastructure" (Sheth, 2011), and typically has a huge population base and rising per capita income (Reinartz et al., 2011). As a result, we must reconsider core marketing assumptions (e.g., market segmentation), marketing perspective, guiding strategy, and marketing practice (Sheth, 2011).

We only investigate the Indian setting to provide context for our work. In terms of population, India is one of the world's largest markets, with a sizable middle-class population and rising income levels. Furthermore, the retailing landscape in EMs is characterized by the coexistence of organized and unorganized retail, with retail in India, for example, consisting of 93 percent unorganized retailers and 7 percent organized retailers (Gupta & Ramachandran, 2021). Because small, unorganized retailers dominate the country, customer-centricity in organized retail faces numerous obstacles and challenges, including a lack of infrastructure and technological adoption by retailers. Despite these obstacles, leading Indian retailers are moving toward organized customer-centric retailing. Changes in marketing strategy are assisting this development, which has implications for operations. As a result, India is an intriguing setting for our study, providing rich insights. This book examines the Indian market, where customer-centricity is beginning to emerge in organized retail. This book identifies the critical issue that keeps retailers from becoming more customer-centric. This is primarily due to a strategic mismatch in retail marketing strategy. To overcome these barriers or strategic mismatches, the book provides strategic takeaways and tools for customer-centricity, which is driven by matching retail strategy with consumer preference factors. This book covers many approaches, including structural equation modeling and the Analytical Hierarchical Process, informed by primary data and practice and theoretical developments driven by the existing literature.

Chapters in This Book

The following two chapters provided an overview of the concepts of customer-centricity and organized retailing. The subsequent chapters are organized primarily around strategy, which focuses on the antecedents of patronage intention and how they relate to consumers' shopping motivations in the context of organized retail. As a result, a more practical approach to customer segmentation is provided and evidence of the moderating effect of consumer demographics is conceptualized in the form of the Shopping Motivation and Patronage Intention (SMPI) Model. That is, we focused on comprehending the consumer side. This is followed by a study on why retailers' counter-strategies fail. This chapter is a continuation of the previous chapter in that knowing the antecedents of patronage intention is insufficient; thus, it untangles the strategic misalignment between consumers' preferred factors and retailers' counter-strategies toward customer-centric organized retail. That is, we also focused on understanding the retailer (strategy) side. This series of chapters eventually delves into the antecedents of consumers' patronage intention, the role of shopping motivation, and why retailers should care to rethink and match their counter-strategies to the consumers' expectations.

In practice, however, the chapters all consider the book's central theme and thus touch on various points related to customer-centric organized retail, as it is impossible to discuss only one element of customer-centric organized retail without referring to other areas. All elements of customer-centric organized retailing implementation, from customer segmentation strategy to retailer counter-strategy, are interconnected and coexist. As a result, it is unavoidable that many components and actors will be considered when investigating a specific aspect of customer-centric organized retail. When the decision is made to implement customer-centricity, the change in strategy results in changes in marketing and operations, which is not surprising but challenging to implement in practice. This book, the result of a series of expert consultations and empirical studies, contributes to our understanding of customer-centric organized retail in a broader context and provides guidelines to implement customer-centricity in organized retail in practice more efficiently.

Based on the extant literature and chapters in this book, it is possible to recognize that there is a discrepancy between the implementation of customer-centricity in organized retailing and the idealistic view of customer-centricity in organized retail, as evidenced by our study, which requires careful rethinking and the discrepancy needs to be reduced, and such efforts will determine the future of organized retailing. We can see that customer-centricity in organized retail is not uniform worldwide, with some markets and sectors leading the way and others attempting to follow suit. As a result, future research should cover more diverse economic settings, both locally and globally relevant. Customer-centricity in organized retail can be developed for various customer segments, with different solutions tailored to the specific needs of each segment. This need may become even more apparent in future studies that compare emerging markets to developed markets. Customer-centricity in organized retailing is rising in both markets, but distinct customer demographics and cultural contexts differ between markets and within them, particularly in large countries like India. We are unable to investigate all such contexts at this time fully. This book is a step toward increasing our understanding of customer-centricity in organized retailing in an emerging market as an emerging phenomenon, emphasizing the importance of retailers rethinking and matching their counter-strategies to match consumers' expectations to ensure the implementation of customer-centricity.

Our book is handy for EM retailers who: (1) want to adopt a customer-centric strategy in an organized retail setting, (2) want to become customer-centric but are not sure where they are going wrong or why they are not getting the desired results, and where they need to focus, or (3) have decided to adopt a customer-centric strategy but need guidance on the specific gap in their current retailing strategy in terms of addressing customer expectations. Our findings highlight the importance of organized EM retailers understanding current consumer expectations and aligning retail strategy toward customer-centricity for EM retailers. Our proposed strategic tools give organized retailers clear guidance on the specific strategies they should use to derive insights to help them achieve their desired customer-centricity. The strategic guidelines can assist retailers in allocating resources to relevant marketing strategies and capability development to become more customer-centric and improve their financial and non-financial firm performance.

References

Ben-Shabat, H., Moriarty, M., Peterson, E., & Kassack, J. (2016). *Emerging market retailing in 2030: Future scenarios and the $5.5 trillion swing—Article—España—Kearney*. https://www.es.kearney.com/consumer-retail/article/?/a/emerging-market-retailing-in-2030-future-scenarios-and-the-5-5-trillion-swing

Gummesson, E. (2008). Customer centricity: Reality or a wild goose chase? *European Business Review, 20*(4), 315–330. https://doi.org/10.1108/09555340810886594

Gupta, S., & Ramachandran, D. (2021). Emerging market retail: Transitioning from a product-centric to a customer-centric approach. *Journal of Retailing, 97*(4), 597–620. https://doi.org/10.1016/j.jretai.2021.01.008

Inversini, A., De Carlo, M., & Masiero, L. (2020). The effects of customer-centricity in hospitality. *International Journal of Hospitality Management, 86*, 102436. https://doi.org/10.1016/j.ijhm.2019.102436

Lamberti, L. (2013). Customer centricity: The construct and the operational antecedents. *Journal of Strategic Marketing, 21*(7), 588–612. https://doi.org/10.1080/0965254X.2013.817476

Latinovic, Z., & Chatterjee, S. C. (2019). Customer centricity in the digital age. *MIT Sloan Management Review, 60*(4), 0_1–0_2.

Lee, J.-Y., Sridhar, S., Henderson, C. M., & Palmatier, R. W. (2015). Effect of customer-centric structure on long-term financial performance. *Marketing Science, 34*(2), 250–268. https://doi.org/10.1287/mksc.2014.0878

Morgan, B. (2019). Of the most customer-centric companies. *Forbes*. https://www.forbes.com/sites/blakemorgan/2019/06/30/100-of-the-most-customer-centric-companies

OECD (Organization for Economic Co-operation and Development). (2018). *Economic outlook for Southeast Asia, China and India 2019: Towards smart urban transportation*. https://www.oecd-ilibrary.org/content/publication/saeo-2019-en

Reinartz, W., Dellaert, B., Krafft, M., Kumar, V., & Varadarajan, R. (2011). Retailing innovations in a globalizing retail market environment. *Journal of Retailing, 87*, S53–S66. https://doi.org/10.1016/j.jretai.2011.04.009

Selden, L., & MacMillan, I. C. (2006). Manage customer-centric innovation—systematically. *Harvard Business Review, 84*(4), 108–116; 149.

Shah, D., Rust, R. T., Parasuraman, A., Staelin, R., & Day, G. S. (2006). The path to customer centricity. *Journal of Service Research, 9*(2), 113–124. https://doi.org/10.1177/1094670506294666

Sheth, J. N. (2011). Impact of emerging markets on marketing: Rethinking existing perspectives and practices. *Journal of Marketing, 75*(4), 166–182. https://doi.org/10.1509/jmkg.75.4.166

Sheth, J. N., Sisodia, R. S., & Sharma, A. (2000). The antecedents and consequences of customer-centric marketing. *Journal of the Academy of Marketing Science, 28*(1), 55–66. https://doi.org/10.1177/0092070300281006

Social Searcher. (2021). *Social buzz—Free social mentions search and monitoring.* http://www.social-searcher.com. https://www.social-searcher.com/social-buzz/?q5=customer+centricity

Wagner, C., & Majchrzak, A. (2006). Enabling customer-centricity using wikis and the wiki way. *Journal of Management Information Systems, 23*(3), 17–43. https://doi.org/10.2753/MIS0742-1222230302

CHAPTER 2

Customer-Centricity: The Quest for Customer Focus

Introduction

It is not uncommon in marketing to see concepts proposed with no precise definition, leaving it up to the readers to understand and evaluate the topic's essence. It is frequently observed that a thin line separates the proposed concepts from those found during the journey through relevant literature (Varadarajan, 2010, p. 138). Similarly, the concept of customer-centricity has gained traction in recent years. A universally accepted definition of this concept has yet to be established, and there are numerous parallels between customer-centricity and a few other existing marketing concepts.

Customer-centricity is a marketing concept that has generated considerable debate in the literature (Lamberti, 2013). However, major companies such as IBM and Best Buy have recently prioritized customer-centricity to gain a competitive advantage. In response to environmental turbulence and global competition, some of the world's most influential consulting firms, such as McKinsey, emphasize the need for companies to adopt a customer-centric approach. Marketing scholars have long referred to customer-centricity (e.g., Tersine & Harvey, 1998) as an incumbent, if not inescapable, business challenge. Moreover, even though numerous researchers and practitioners have repeatedly emphasized evidence of how critical and visionary the concept of customer-centricity is, the

© The Author(s), under exclusive license to Springer Nature Singapore Pte Ltd. 2023
M. K. Dash et al., *Customer-Centricity in Organized Retailing*, https://doi.org/10.1007/978-981-19-3593-0_2

paradigm shift from traditional product-centric practices to customer-centric practices is either ignored or difficult for many organizations. A literature review reveals that neither a common understanding of the term "customer-centricity" nor sufficient evidence of why customer-centricity fails to be implemented in its idealist view has emerged thus far. As a result, it is unclear how to implement customer-centricity, nor where it might go wrong. The latter, on the other hand, is covered in subsequent chapters. In this section, we will concentrate on the concept of customer-centricity.

Although the term appears self-explanatory, customer-centricity is not as self-explanatory as it appears, as explained in the later sections of this chapter. Even a few years ago, literature on customer-centricity reflected the state of the marketing concept until the late 1980s, when it was little more than a business philosophy or a definitive policy statement. "Marketing is seeing your business through the eyes of the customers," wrote Peter Drucker in the 1950s, who was a leading management thinker in America until he died in 2005. When customer-centricity reached the public sector in the 1980s, patients became customers, students and parents became customers of the school, and so on (Gummesson, 2008). The concepts' boundaries were gradually pushed even further. Then, in the early 1900s, Gustav Dalén, the CEO of AGA and a Swedish Nobel Laureate, said, "Solve the customers' problem. Give them possibilities to increase profitability, security, and quality in their operations. Help them introduce new and better technology." Today, however, we can define customer-centricity as a business that operates with strategies and workflow designed with the customer as the focal point. Customer-centricity, in Peter Drucker's definition, is "a strategy that aligns a company's development and delivery of its products and services with the current and future needs of a select group of customers to maximize their long-term financial value to the firm" (Drucker, 2020).

So, while customer-centricity is not entirely new, it has become more refined in recent years; however, how well do we handle it today? Though the boards of various large corporations claim that they are flourishing in implementing and maintaining customer-centric products or services, the last mile reality in most cases differs significantly from what the executives plan and believe is being done. Though senior executives claim that their organizations are customer-centric, this is not being delivered to the customer, complicating matters further. Though there is a clear breach of expectation and delivery, companies'/organizations' efforts to bridge the gaps are commendable; however, proper pathway guidance is required to put things into perspective.

Customer-centricity is rapidly gaining traction in the business world. In just a decade (from 2008 to 2018), the number of searches for the term "customer-centricity" more than doubled (Habel et al., 2020). As a result, several top business schools and universities, are now emphasizing the concept of customer-centricity to prepare their students, who will most likely be future business leaders, for a world of rapid change in terms of customer needs, wants, and how businesses can address them. This book is intended to address this pathway to assist companies, organizations, senior executives, and upcoming business leaders who are currently students in building or transforming themselves into customer-centric organizations. The remainder of this chapter is written to explain what customer-centricity is and is not and its various dimensions.

1. What is customer-centricity?

What it is, why it is, whom it applies to, and whom it implies are all things to consider when it comes to customer-centricity. Though several definitions aptly define customer-centricity depending on the context in which it is used, customer-centricity is defined as keeping the customer at the center of attention and designing various marketing and selling techniques around the customer. Customer-centricity may appear to be a simple and obvious phenomenon but implementing business principles is one of the most complicated and challenging. Even though numerous studies have potentially demonstrated that customer-centricity is the best principle that can be followed for the best and incredibly efficient outputs for most businesses, according to Fader and Winer (2012), a large number of well-known and well-run companies are still nowhere near accepting or adopting the principle of customer-centricity despite its proven benefits. In his well-known book on customer-centricity, he mentioned "Customer-centricity concentrates on the right customers to gain a strategic advantage "that none of the world's largest and most well-known corporations, such as Apple, Starbucks, and Walmart, are genuinely customer-centric.

Companies want to maintain customer-centricity in the face of increasing technological advancements and a shift toward online information-seeking and shopping environments. Bose (2002) suitably identified and emphasized how business orientation has evolved. It was purely production growth-focused in the 1900s, then scale growth-focused until the 1950s. Furthermore, by the early 2000s, it had shifted to a marketing-driven focus, and it has now been transformed into a customer-centric focus. Perhaps, in 2020, technological advancements and the shift in shopping behavior resulting from technological advancements are to blame for the companies' interest in customer-centricity. Though the concept of customer-centricity appears to be reasonably obvious and appealing, it has only recently received its due attention following the digitalization revolution. A noticeable shift and race of companies toward maintaining excellent relationships with customers, taking feedback, enhancing customer experience, and so on is now encouraging them to stick to a customer-centric way of operating businesses.

In many cases, customer-centricity is a variable that takes shape according to the orientation of the business in which it is applied. Bailey and Jensen (2006) define customer-centricity as aligning your organization's resources to effectively respond to the customer's ever-changing needs while building a mutually profitable relationship. Customers' needs are rapidly evolving as a result of rapid changes in technology and comfort expectations. Therefore, to meet customers' needs, businesses must quickly analyze customer needs and mold themselves accordingly. The three essential pillars of customer-centricity are,

1. To understand the customer.
2. Improving the business according to the feedback.
3. Designing the experience.

2. A brief history of customer-centricity:

Whether addressed or not, customer-centricity has existed since the beginning of the selling and buying trade. If one understands the basic concept of customer-centricity, this may be related. It is nothing more than keeping the customer's needs, satisfaction, requirements, and overall customer perspective as the most critical factor. Since the beginning of selling and buying, the entire concept of selling has revolved, whether intentionally or unintentionally, around the customer. Designing and running a business around the customer is one aspect of customer-centricity, and it is essentially the idea behind starting a business in the first place. Customer-centricity is, at its most basic, a seller matching the buyer's demands. According to Bailey and Jensen (2006), the concept of customer-centricity has been present in various forms since humankind has known to trade, albeit not with the same intensity. Eventually, as industrialization progressed, so-called supermarkets and showrooms became more concerned with profit than meeting customers' needs, in contrast to how the business used to be when it was on a much smaller scale. For example, a baker in a street shop used to bake bread that matched the tastes of those customers who regularly visited his/her shop. In contrast, a supermarket, which has now replaced that small bakery business, does not have the same relationship with its customers. Thus, the customers who regularly visit the store need and thus make bread that does not match their customer's tastes. This brief example demonstrates how customer-centricity might be lacking.

If not the term, Drucker (1954) introduced the concept of putting the customer first rather than the sale, stating in his book "The Practice of Management" that "it is the customer who determines what a business is, what it produces, and whether it will prosper." Lester Wunderman is widely regarded as the person who pioneered customer-centricity. According to Holder (2008), the term "direct marketing," from which the concept of customer-centricity arose. Before Wunderman proposed direct marketing, marketers focused on reaching many potential customers, which has since shifted to reaching individual users through one-on-one channels such as emails, phone calls, etc. As a result, customer-centricity has increased.

With the advancement of ICT, customers are exposed to a more significant number of options to choose from. To compete, businesses must focus on customer needs more than ever before. In a world where businesses are rushing to get their products and services to market, assuming that one needs to make customers realize what they need, a few businesses attempt to work the other way around and ensure that what their customers need has stood out.

3. Importance of customer-centricity:

For a company to be successful in today's world, it must embrace customer-centricity and focus its capabilities on improving customer-centric competencies. He also mentioned that the faster a company adapts to customer-centricity, the better its competitive advantage and those left behind will scramble for a competitive necessity. Customers are the heart of any business and are therefore critical to its survival. Given this, businesses must transition to a customer-centric mindset as soon as possible. A satisfied customer is the ultimate goal of any business, and a positive customer experience is the most critical source of competitive advantage.

In the case of customer relationships, the adage "knowledge is wealth" is apt. The more information one has about their customers' expectations and needs, the better one can derive knowledge to improve the customer experience, which is critical for any product or service. Therefore, customer-centricity can provide a significant competitive advantage to businesses, mainly when most businesses are still focused on product-centricity.

The importance of customer-centricity has always been there. Many companies have religiously followed a customer-centric approach for a long time; however, the importance of customer-centricity has drastically increased in recent times. There could be several reasons why customer-centricity has become so popular in recent years, with the main one being the rise of e-commerce. The electronic medium-based buying and selling have given customers more leverage to realize further what they want, how they want to deal with companies, and, to a lesser extent, how they want the companies to behave and conduct business. The customer now owns the market and even the businesses rather than the business. Another important reason for the rise of customer-centricity is the globalization of the customer. Growth in the freedom to buy, impressive knowledge-sharing and acquiring abilities, and the ability to compare numerous companies and strategies could be reasons for customer-centricity. Customer-centricity is very important to match all of these aspects.

4. Building customer-centricity:

Even though the concept of customer-centricity is not new, and despite its well-established benefits, many businesses are finding it challenging to align themselves with the customer-centric paradigm. The purpose of this book is to help readers understand what customer-centricity is and how to create a customer-centric culture. Let us now try to understand how to implement customer-centricity along these lines. Furthermore, we will go over the step-by-step process of developing customer-centricity.

a. *Maintaining an excellent customer relationship*:

Knowing your customer and connecting with them is unquestionably the most critical factor for any business, regardless of size or stature. A strong relationship with customers is required to build a culture of customer-centricity. There are numerous ways to improve customer relationships found up to this point, one of which is to collect customer feedback regularly. In this digitalized network-driven era, feedback collection has become much more efficient and, in some ways, simple. The term "easy" does not refer to the ease with which feedback is collected; instead, it refers to the ease with which feedback is requested, as feedback is now collected via social media, emails, SMS, and other means. Customer relationship management entails more than just formally connecting with a customer; it also includes strategies to retain customers.

b. *Align the mission of the company to customer-centric*:

Customer-centricity should be recognized as a way of doing business and a way of dealing with customers. However, even before adopting the culture, a company and its employees must first adapt it as a philosophy or execution. When customer-centricity becomes ingrained in the company culture, it shifts its business policy and alters its business strategy. "Put your customers first," an old but still relevant adage, is strictly enforced. Any organization that wants to embed a customer-centric culture must start from the ground up, with mission and vision statements centered on the customer. Companies that are already established should reframe their mission and vision statements to emphasize a customer-centric approach.

In many cases, a severe problem arises: the employees intended for customer service or, in general, are given way below-the-belt powers to make any decisions. This adversely affects the customer after purchase satisfaction and immensely affects the company. Therefore, it is essential to give the employees the proper authority to make appropriate decisions to address their needs. Customers must always reach the company with ease. Companies must always ensure that the customers who reach them are delighted with the services they receive, whether before or after purchase.

c. *Asking and understanding what customer wants*:

There is no better way to find out what your customers want than to ask them. Communicating efficiently with the target customer group will provide an idea of customer needs and increase customer loyalty, thus killing two birds with one stone.

d. *Employee hiring to board member's setup being keen about customer-centric attitude*:

Human resources working in an organization have an impact on the organization's overall culture. As previously discussed, the customer-centric culture must be adapted and followed by the owner to the cleaner. Only then can a company be considered an actual customer-centric organization. The most critical grassroots work a company must do is hire the right people who perfectly match their mission statement (setting the mission according to customer-centricity is significant, as discussed before). Employees and the company's top executives must instill the culture of customer-centricity; only then will lower-level employees follow it effectively. According to an adage, "the citizen's culture is mostly influenced by the King's," so the leadership must have a properly customer-centric attitude to make the entire company customer-centric.

e. *Employee participation*:

A customer-centric culture is not limited to a specific group of employees. As previously discussed, the entire company must shift toward customer-centricity, addressing the customer's needs and desires; the entire

2 CUSTOMER-CENTRICITY: THE QUEST FOR CUSTOMER FOCUS

company must work for the customer. Frequently misunderstood as the responsibility of the customer service department, customer-centricity is the owner's responsibility to the company's cleaner. A company must adopt an all-inclusive approach to customer-centricity. There are companies where the top-level executives frequently interact with customers through customer support departments. Other companies go a step further and let their engineers or core policymakers directly interact with customers to get a firsthand idea of what a customer is going through, and what their needs and wants are.

5. Product-centricity vs. Customer-centricity:

Now that we have defined customer-centricity, let us look at the distinction between it and its twin concept, "product-centricity." Product-centricity is a concept that is currently widely used by companies that do not take a customer-centric approach. While customer-centric is about selling products and services tailored to customers' needs and expectations, product-centric is the polar opposite. Product-centric businesses focus on simply selling their products and making money while paying little attention to what their target customers want. Product-centric businesses do not simply know who their customers are and what they require; instead, they are all about selling their products, emphasizing what they have, and creating demand for their products in any way possible. According to Fader and Toms (2018), "Many commercial enterprises still take a product-centric approach to business, which derives value creation from alone proposition: selling as many products and services to many faceless, nameless customers as possible."

To put it simply, product-centricity extols the characteristics and features of the product, whereas customer-centricity focuses on how a product can add value to the customer. A product-centric coffee brand, for example, would likely advertise that there are no added chemicals and that the amount of caffeine in each serving is the same, that they use BPA (bisphenol A)-free packaging, and so on. In contrast, a customer-centric coffee brand would likely proclaim how their coffee increases productivity, how caffeine can help as a pre-training product, or how refreshing a morning can be with their coffee.

When a product is sold to a customer based on its features and characteristics, it is product-centric. The entire focus is on what the product contains, with little emphasis on whether or not it addresses the customer's needs or addresses the customer's needs. In the coffee brand example given above, the product-centric coffee brand has emphasized how their coffee has various features and characteristics with little to no consideration of why that coffee is suitable for a customer and how it can help them improve their being.

A customer-centric product is sold to address the customer's needs rather than satisfy the norms of upgrading the product to get in a new product every specific period. As defined by Peter Fader, author of the well-known book "Customer Centricity: Focus on the Right Customers for Strategic Advantage," customer-centricity is all about designing everything else to be in sync with the customer. In our coffee brand example, the customer-centric brand began with the customer and worked backward. Instead of promoting and showcasing the features of the coffee, they have focused on demonstrating how their coffee adds value, excitement, and productivity to the lives of their customers. Aside from that, they take customer feedback and use it to improve their product.

Shah et al. (2006) have given an in-depth comparison of product-centric and customer-centric approaches (See, https://www.theseus.fi/handle/10024/73331 for the comparison between the product-centric approach and the customer-centric approach).

6. Challenges in implementing customer-centricity:

As previously discussed, most businesses currently practice a product-centric approach; however, shifting to a customer-centric approach is not an easy overnight phenomenon; it requires much effort. A lot of revenue flow must be diverted to it. H&M is an example of a company that has been successful for a long time. However, most businesses have peaks and valleys; Ericsson is one (Gummesson, 2008). Many businesses adapt well to change and emerge as winners, while others become stuck in their previous success. It is essential when significant changes are required. When these changes are required, one of the challenges is the profitability of customer-centricity, which is frequently questioned by management. They are concerned that customer-centricity will cost money but bring in no revenue (Gummesson, 2008). According to Shah et al. (2006), the four main constraints that challenge customer-centricity implementation are as follows:

1. Organizational culture
2. Organizational structure
3. Processes
4. Financial metrics.

Employees and their ethics have a significant impact on the company's culture. Over the years, companies have trained their employees to deal with their clients to make individual gains (such as bonuses) and the company's profit, which has made the employees very skeptical about knowledge-sharing with their peers. As discussed in previous sections of the chapter, knowledge-sharing is critical for maintaining customer-centricity. Given this culture of dealing with businesses in a self-centered manner, shifting to a customer-centric approach is extremely difficult. Employees' and senior-level executives' and board members' approaches to organizational problems significantly impact the organizations' approach. In simple terms, because companies have traditionally taken a product-centric approach, a complete shift in mindset and work pattern must mobilize the customer-centric approach in the organization, which is a considerable challenge.

The organization's structure is heavily influenced by the hierarchy and the individuals in leadership positions and their activities. In addition, the deeply rooted incentives in a company's product-centric environment are vastly different from those in a customer-centric environment. As a result, the entire organizational structure must align with the organization's new interest, a customer-centric approach. According to Day (1999), any effort to improve alignment entails balancing numerous competing forces. The challenge of shifting from product-centric to customer-centric stems from the fact that functional differences are deeply rooted in various aspects such as incentives, backgrounds and interests, time scales, and task priorities.

Transformational changes in an organization from an existing product-centric approach to a novel customer-centric approach necessitate significant revenue investments. As a result, financial metrics must be seriously considered during the transformation. This is one of the most significant barriers that any organization may face when transitioning from product-centricity to customer-centricity. However, according to Shah et al. (2006), calculating the financial investments made in transforming an organization from product-centric to customer-centric is difficult because the target output is generally intangible, such as loyalty, and customer satisfaction.

7. Cases of customer-centricity:

We have talked and learned a bit about customer-centricity, how it works, the challenges, and so on. This section will look at truly customer-centric companies and how they do it and learn about their success stories.

Amazon, the world's e-commerce leader and a behemoth in its own right, is one of the most customer-centric corporations. The company's vision is the most customer-centric we have seen in recent years. Amazon's vision statement is "We seek to become the world's most customer-centric company; to build a place where people can come to find and discover anything they might want to buy online." Because of its dedication to its customers, the company has become one of the world's leaders in e-commerce. Jeff Bezos, the company's CEO, is well known for his enthusiasm for customers and for learning about their expectations. As discussed in previous sections of this chapter, one of the most critical attributes for establishing and maintaining customer-centricity is its culture. Amazon employees from all levels of the organization spend time with their customers via the service desk. The company requires all managers, including the CEO, to spend at least two days every two years at the customer service desk to understand the customers' needs and what problems they are experiencing. This allows them to gain firsthand knowledge of what needs to be done to get closer to their customers. Consider how well they will perform once they learn directly from their customers what they expect from the company.

Zappos—an apparel company that sells clothing, shoes, and other accessories—is an excellent example of how customer-centricity can increase its popularity among its customers. The company's phone number is listed in block letters on its home page, and they can be reached 24 hours a day, seven days a week. In addition, the first words on their website are "customer service," indicating their commitment to a customer-centric culture.

Tony Hsieh, CEO of Zappos, says, "If it is something that creates a great customer experience, choose to do it because we believe that in the long run, little things that keep the customer in mind will end up paying short dividends." He also said about how they make sure of owning a tremendous service-focused culture; he says if you get the culture right, then many amazing things happen on their own. Also, to be observed with Zappos is how they spend their money enhancing the customer's experience. They provide "free shipping," yes, they consider the shipping costs a part of marketing expenses, making customers more attracted to the brand and feel much more aligned with the company. In the words of CEO, Hsieh "Many customers will order five different pairs of shoes, try them on with five different outfits in the comfort of their living rooms, and then send back the ones that do not fit or they do not like - free of charge. The additional shipping costs are expensive for us, but we view those costs as a marketing expense". Zappos does many things to stick to customer-centric culture in their organization and is a true example of a customer-centric organization.

Conclusion

Customer-centricity is a much-needed intervention in the retail space, but also one must understand that the shift to customer-centricity is very complex and time-consuming. However, step-by-step implementation of a customer-centric approach can be of meaningful help to businesses. Though the challenges of implementing the customer-centricity approach in a business are observably high, it is also evident that the long-term good it brings is worth it.

The business's true potential in terms of bagging customers exponentially increases with the proper implementation of customer-centricity. As discussed in the chapter, many well-known companies worldwide are racing toward customer-centricity to create an edge in the market and substantial competitive advantage. Given the perks of adapting to customer-centricity, it is to be understood that implementation is a complex phenomenon with a plethora of hurdles. The complexity increases with the level of product-centricity intensity existing in the system; the more the companies' culture is aligned toward product-centricity, the more it becomes challenging to shift to customer-centricity. Perhaps the new or yet-to-be-incubated companies have a considerable advantage in this space of adapting to customer-centricity over the established ones.

It is to be noted that customer-centricity is a multi-layered simultaneous adaption principle. Customer-centricity has to be adapted at every business level, from the chairman to the janitor. The challenges in the organization and structure are to be appropriately aligned to the customer-centricity to adapt to the new culture efficiently. Finances are another prominent factor in the implementation of customer-centricity, the change of the complete setup of an already running system includes unexpected costs, and that is one of the reasons why the new companies must understand the value of customer-centricity and adapt it at the beginning so that they grow around this culture.

REFERENCES

Bailey, C., & Jensen, K. (2006). Customer advocacy. *Customer Centricity white paper* (pp. 1–30). Customer Centricity, Inc.

Bose, R. (2002). Customer relationship management: Key components for IT success. *Industrial Management and Data Systems, 102*(2), 89–97. https://doi.org/10.1108/02635570210419636

Day, G. (1999). Aligning organizational structure to the market. *Business Strategy Review, 10*(3), 33–46. https://doi.org/10.1111/1467-8616.00109

Drucker, P. (1954). F. *The practice of management*. Harpers.

Drucker, P. F. (2020). Economic realities and enterprise strategy. In *Modern Japanese organization and decision-making* (pp. 228–248). University of California Press.

Fader, P., & Toms, S. (2018). *The customer centricity playbook: Implement a winning strategy driven by customer lifetime value*. Wharton School Press.

Fader, P. S., & Winer, R. S. (2012). Introduction to the special issue on the emergence and impact of user-generated content. *Marketing Science, 31*(3), 369–371. https://doi.org/10.1287/mksc.1120.0715

Gummesson, E. (2008). Customer centricity: Reality or a wild goose chase? *European Business Review, 20*(4), 315–330. https://doi.org/10.1108/09555340810886594

Habel, J., Kassemeier, R., Alavi, S., Haaf, P., Schmitz, C., & Wieseke, J. (2020). When do customers perceive customer centricity? The role of a firm's and salespeople's customer orientation. *Journal of Personal Selling and Sales Management, 40*(1), 25–42. https://doi.org/10.1080/08853134.2019.1631174

Holder, D. (2008). What do we mean by direct, data and digital marketing? In *The marketing book* (pp. 410–428). Routledge.

Lamberti, L. (2013). Customer centricity: The construct and the operational antecedents. *Journal of Strategic Marketing, 21*(7), 588–612. https://doi.org/10.1080/0965254X.2013.817476

Shah, D., Rust, R. T., Parasuraman, A., Staelin, R., & Day, G. S. (2006). The path to customer centricity. *Journal of Service Research, 9*(2), 113–124. https://doi.org/10.1177/1094670506294666

Tersine, R., & Harvey, M. (1998). Global customerization of markets has arrived! *European Management Journal, 16*(1), 79–90. https://doi.org/10.1016/S0263-2373(97)00076-5

Varadarajan, R. (2010). Strategic marketing and marketing strategy: Domain, definition, fundamental issues and foundational premises. *Journal of the Academy of Marketing Science, 38*(2), 119–140. https://doi.org/10.1007/s11747-009-0176-7

CHAPTER 3

Organized Retailing: A Brief Introduction

Introduction

Emerging markets (EMs) organized retailers currently make up a small portion of the fragmented retail landscape. Due to demographic and socioeconomic shifts and their desire for a better shopping experience, EM consumers are increasingly settling toward organized retail. To provide a better customer experience, organized retailers are changing their value chain (upstream and downstream) activities (Gupta & Ramachandran, 2021). Compared to 85 percent in the United States and 40 percent and 55 percent in Thailand and Malaysia, organized retail in India is negligible, accounting for only 4 percent of the retail sector. However, the retail industry has proven to be one of the most promising job-creating sectors, with massive revenue-generating potential, over the years. Organized retailing has emerged as a fast-paced and dynamic industry due to intense competition caused by marketers' entry into the organized retailing space.

To date, most organized EM retailers have continued to take a product-centric approach, focusing on their best-selling products and leveraging technological innovations to attract customers (Gupta & Ramachandran, 2021). Retailers continue to send out standardized push notifications to all customers without considering their unique and varied needs. Such ineffective marketing strategies do more harm than

© The Author(s), under exclusive license to Springer Nature
Singapore Pte Ltd. 2023
M. K. Dash et al., *Customer-Centricity in Organized Retailing*,
https://doi.org/10.1007/978-981-19-3593-0_3

good to businesses. Customers are indifferent to and enraged by retailers' marketing strategies and actions resulting from such strategies that distance the company from customer-centricity (Gupta & Ramachandran, 2021). Understanding consumer expectations through surveys or other forms of analytics across value-chain activities can be helpful in this regard; however, the use of such strategies is limited and, in most cases, rudimentary. Although some organized retailers employ customer-centric marketing strategies, they fail to realize the value of customer-centricity because they fail to consider consolidated consumer preferences and develop retail strategies to match them. Retail marketers' lack of understanding of strategic tools limits their ability to provide customers with the services and products they want and assistance to improve the overall experience. The following chapters will propose a method for understanding what consumers expect and what retailers should deliver to meet those expectations. However, in this chapter, we will only discuss the concept of organized retailing.

What is Organized Retailing?

The retail industry has dominated the revenue-generating spectrum all over the world. However, there is still a disparity in how retailing is carried out. Organized and unorganized retailing are the opposite poles of the retail spectrum that are conveniently followed based on location, requirement, and adaptability capabilities within a geographic boundary.

Organized retailing is retailing that is subject to strict regulations and laws. The business activities between a business and a customer or a business activity between two businesses in an organized retailing are carried out by licensed players required to pay taxes and follow the laws of the government.

> *Organized retailing refers to trading activities undertaken by licensed retailers (e.g., supermarkets, corporate-backed hypermarkets, and retail chains). By contrast, unorganized retailing is characterized by small neighborhood stores selling groceries (mom-and-pop stores, also called Kirana shops in India).*
>
> Jerath et al. (2016)

A certain set of specific requirements for an organized retail business must meet. An organized retail sector must meet those minimum requirements, such as being a registered private company with payroll employees, human resource contracts, government regulations, and laws protecting employees. Organized retailing practicing businesses serve customers in a very different way than unorganized ones. The significant difference between an organized retail store and an unorganized retail store could be the size of the business. Usually, the unorganized retail stores are the small mom-and-pop stores run by family members confined to a good real estate establishment. The financing of these unorganized stores is significantly less than the organized ones, and the shopping feel it offers to the customers is relatively low. Loyalty is usually observed to be strong in the unorganized sector. Perhaps it is the relationship they share with their customers and the geographical advantage as often the unorganized stores are close to their regular customers. According to Child et al. (2015), the stores located in the neighborhood of customers are aware of their preferences due to the frequent visits of the customers, which can develop the relationship between the seller and the customer and offer personalized services to them.

In contrast, an organized retail practicing business has a much more persistent approach to running a business. An organized retail store's salient difference from an unorganized business is that it serves multiple times more people/customers in a given period than an unorganized space. To meet the customer inflow and to handle them. The organized stores have a more extensive real estate establishment where they operate, and to run such organizations, the finances included are pretty high. The involvement of governments is higher in the organized retail sector in terms of regulations and tax collections, whereas it is minimal to nil in the unorganized. The prominent differences between both sectors are listed in Table 3.1.

Organized Retailing in Emerging Markets

Across the globe, the retail sector has accounted for a sizable portion of revenue generation and rising productivity. Many developed and developing countries have seen the retail sector impact their economies through the goods and service sectors. The retail industry makes a significant contribution to a country's GDP. In 2013, total retail sales in the United States surpassed $4.5 trillion. Even in a developing country like

Table 3.1 Difference between organized and unorganized retail sectors

Organized retail sector	Unorganized retail sector
Regulated by government and employment terms	No regulations from the government and no employment terms
Governed by acts (e.g., minimum wage act)	No government acts
The organized retail sector has employees with regular salaries	The unorganized retail sector generally has daily wage workers
Job security for employees	No job security for employees
Usually established in a more prominent real estate	Usually are small mom-and-pop stores
Serves a few hundred to a few thousand customers daily	The daily customers are very few
The establishment has proper channels and procedures	Easy to establish
Organized retail stores must pay taxes	No tax

Source Bhasin (2021)

India, retailing is worth approximately $500 billion and accounts for 37 percent of the country's GDP (Kohli & Bhagwati, 2011).

Retailing is not the same in every country. According to Jerath et al. (2016), organized retailing dominates the retailing landscape in most developed countries, whereas unorganized retailing is the dominant format in emerging economies. Organized retailing is now practiced in a wide range of countries, including both developed and emerging markets. Countries like the United States, India, China, and Indonesia practice organized retailing following their local capabilities. For example, organized retailing is widely practiced in the United States, whereas organized retailing is primarily seen in urban areas in India. Unorganized retailing is prevalent in developing countries.

Unorganized retailing predominates in emerging markets. The small stores set up in a small amount of real estate and serve a small number of customers in their immediate vicinity distinguish features of this type of retail. On the other hand, an organized retail outlet is established significantly larger and researched real estate with all the amenities to attract customers. Every day, it serves between a few hundred and a few thousand customers.

Purchasing from an organized retail store incurs various costs, including time spent planning a trip to the store, driving and parking expenses, and other in-store expenses (Child et al., 2015). The requirement is the most important consideration for customers when choosing between organized and unorganized retail stores. They decide whether they need to visit the store a certain number of times per week or once every few weeks. There is also a significant impact on consumer purchasing behavior depending on whether they visit organized or unorganized stores. Due to the coexistence of organized and unorganized stores, consumers have an edge in buying from an organized store or an unorganized store. However, there is an opportunity cost for choosing either of them. According to Jerath et al. (2016), various factors like the available storage capacity of the consumer and the customized service at an unorganized store in their vicinity can influence the choice of retailer and the quantity purchased. Such factors influence the stability of organized as well as unorganized stores in the market and their ability to decide the pricing.

Several empirical research studies have focused on the impact of large retailer entry, such as Walmart, on consumer purchase behavior (Singh et al., 2006), retail prices, and other aspects of the marketing mix (Ailawadi et al., 2010; Basker, 2005a), and the impact of other retailers' entry and exit (Basker, 2005b; Jia, 2008). In an emerging market, the dynamics of markets are peculiar. For example, in India, a consumer who belongs to the upper-middle class and the lower-middle-class groups were observed to be more responsive to modern retailing and organized retailing when compared to other groups such as higher-income groups, poor, or below-the-poverty-line people. According to Sudhir and Talukdar (2015), modernization influenced by information technology enhancements is not well appreciated by Indian retailers due to the limited transparency for regulators into their operations, at the cost of not expanding optimally.

In their attempt to provide novel insights into the interplay between organized and unorganized retailing, Jerath et al. (2016) have some exciting details regarding the correlation between organized and unorganized markets. Their research found that the rise of organized retailing will result in a few unorganized retailers leaving the market. However, they claim that the surviving retailers might charge a higher price to make a higher post-entry profit than the organized retailer's scenario. This phenomenon is a result of the entry of an efficient and organized retailer in the market, which has, in turn, reduced the number of unorganized retailers probably due to the inability to withstand the competition and, as a result, overall competition among the surviving unorganized market in the given market space can potentially be reduced. These results from Jerath et al. (2016) agree with the findings in a comprehensive study of developments in Indian retailing by Kohli and Bhagwati (2011), Bhagwati and Panagariya (2013).

Challenges in Organized Retailing in Emerging Markets

In an emerging market, establishing an organized retail sector is nothing less than attempting a paradigm shift in the region's customer buying behavior. However efficiently a company strategizes to take up this challenge, there are a few inevitable challenges it might face in emerging markets. A few of them are listed below;

Government restriction: Governments' restriction on foreign direct investments is one of the significant challenges in emerging markets for establishing the organized retail industry. The government's lack of recognition of organized retail as an industry is the other major cause of the organized retail sector not growing in emerging markets. The nonidentification of the organized retail sector as an industry can barricade the flow of potential investors who would like to invest in the organized retail space.

Real estate: As previously stated, an organized retail store necessitates a larger establishment with better infrastructure than an unorganized retail store. The initial cost of establishment includes the cost of real estate, which may be the most expensive of the initial costs. Government subsidies and simple loan procedures could aid the growth of the organized retail sector.

Competition from the unorganized sector: Unorganized sectors operate on a completely different scale than organized retail stores. Customers in organized retail stores range from weekly to monthly customers and typically shop in bulk. In contrast, customers in unorganized retail stores rely on day-to-day needs and frequent customers who shop significantly fewer quantities. Due to their presence on every corner, unorganized stores have a high likelihood of customers making purchases rather than traveling long distances to purchase from organized stores. For example, in India, slightly more than 90 percent of the retail sector is unorganized, and such conditions are a significant impediment to the operations of organized retail sectors.

Supply chain management: The management of the supply chain is critical for any organized retail store. The supply chain technology used is critical for dealing with stock replenishment and stock upgrade. The efficiency of software has made life easier for organized retailers until some retailers find it challenging to handle the technology, where supply chain issues arise. In addition to technology, logistics management is an essential aspect of supply chain management in organized retailing. Any well-organized retail store must have adequate transportation and storage facilities.

Infrastructure: To a large extent, the logistics of a retail sector depend on the movement of goods. In any be in emerging or developed, roadways are prominently used in the transportation and logistics of goods. Poor infrastructure of the region can significantly affect the mobilizing of the goods which can incur losses and develop the slightest interest in the investors to invest in such markets. Storage facilities are another important factor when it comes to infrastructure. Lack of proper cold storage spaces can hamper the development of food and grocery in the retail industry. A substantial investment in the development of infrastructure is crucial for the organizes retail growth.

Human resource: Organized retailing is all about handling the retail business; unlike in the unorganized sector, organized retail space involves professionals in the day-to-day task. The necessity of a trained workforce can be a challenge faced by organized retail operators. Managing human resources is again a considerable task in itself. The remuneration demand could be high for trained human resources, bringing down the organization's profit-making capacity.

CUSTOMER-CENTRICITY IN ORGANIZED RETAILING

The retail industry's competition is only increasing; thus, retailers must take innovative steps to attract customers. Shifting to organized retailing has helped many retailers increase customer footfall while also increasing sales revenues. However, competition in organized retailing is also increasing, necessitating adopting a new strategy for gaining a competitive advantage. According to Kumar (2008), intense competition among supermarket retailers is becoming saturated, necessitating the players' competitive advantage. In today's hyper-competitive environment, retailers are eying a customer-centric approach to gain a competitive advantage over their rivals; customer-centricity the concept of putting the customer and their needs at the center of all business decisions—has gained traction as a business strategy. According to Walters and Knee (1989), firms that make themselves more appealing to customers than competitors and establish a strategic position in the marketplace can gain a competitive advantage.

The major retail mix elements of a customer-centric strategy are a retail location, merchandise assortment, store design and display (store appearance), and customer service. The non-price attributes essential to a retail customer: are product assortment, convenience, customer service, and experience. In conclusion, it appears clear that customer-centric retail strategies focusing on location, service quality, product assortment, and store ambiance will undoubtedly allow retail firms to grow and profit in the future.

WAYS TO INCREASE CUSTOMER-CENTRICITY IN RETAILING

The customer's journey from choosing the store to exiting with a purchase involves several steps and demands much effort from the marketer's side. From the ambiance to the help and stock availability to the convenience, a store has to manage many aspects to retain a customer. Along these lines, a few ways to increase customer-centricity in today's retail world are discussed below;

1. Soothing customer's shopping experience:

The internet has now come to marketers as a boon. It enables marketers to serve their customers in the comfort of their homes efficiently. Amazon is a classic example of a retailer using technology to remove obstacles and impediments. Many marketers are deploying technology to ease the process of shopping for their customers. From easy and unbelievably quick delivery to the most accessible returns, marketers compete to serve their customers in the best way possible and attract more customers.

2. Enticing the customer:

They are offering a pleasurable experience to the customer based on the analysis of their preferences and behaviors. The product and services when are designed around the interest of the customer, the attraction of such products and services will be high. Technology again plays a significant role in enhancing the customer's experience and offering an attractive experience. Augmented reality, virtual reality, etc., are playing a prominent role in the technology-driven shopping environment. Nike, for instance, uses an augmented reality app that allows shoppers to try on shoes virtually. The usage of technology Is not just confined to online shopping but also in the traditional space. Automated services like controlled temperature, cleaning, inventory management, and delivery are areas where technology is widely used in offline stores.

3. Hiring policy:

As discussed before, professionalism is an essential prerequisite in the organized retail setup. The impression marketers must be convincing to the customer from the very beginning of their shopping experience. The primary interaction with the organization's staff is the crucial one and has to be well organized. To achieve this, the selection of the employees must be made accordingly. The hiring process must include estimating the candidate's customer orientation and to what extent he/she can maintain customer-centricity in the organization.

The shift of retailing from a conventional process to an organized process in emerging markets is happening due to the increase in financial abilities of the people, increase in consumer expectations, etc. This change is necessary for maintaining customer-centricity in organizations because many companies now have learned the advantage of adapting to customer-centricity.

Conclusion

The organized retail segment is a high-potential and promising space for investors in emerging markets. However, it comes with blatant resistance from the unorganized groups who are operating in the same market. Emerging markets have consistently proven to be the ultimate destination for creativity. The organized retail segment represents a new ray of hope for retail marketers seeking a competitive advantage in existing markets. Even though the organized retail sector has proven efficient in many regions, many developing countries lag in formalizing organized retail industries. Marketers and managers can effectively implement customer-centricity if they understand how the organized retail sector works.

The need is to understand how policies can be made to encourage organized setups. It is to be seriously considered that organized retailing streamlines the business and is a considerable income-gaining space to the governments through taxes. Exploring research to evaluate the authorities' abilities to boost the organized retail sector is one of the best ways to promote it.

The customer-centric approach is an addition to the organized retail setup that provides an advantage to retailers facing intense competition or who want to advance the organized retail set up and has a high scope of further research to see how customer-centricity and organized retailing can go hand in hand. Undoubtedly the organized retail sector has a clear competitive advantage over the unorganized sector in customer-centricity implementation.

References

Ailawadi, K. L., Zhang, J., Krishna, A., & Kruger, M. W. (2010). When Wal-Mart enters: How incumbent retailers react and how this affects their sales outcomes. *Journal of Marketing Research, 47*(4), 577–593. https://doi.org/10.1509/jmkr.47.4.577

Basker, E. (2005a). Selling a cheaper mousetrap: Wal-Mart's effect on retail prices. *Journal of Urban Economics, 58*(2), 203–229. https://doi.org/10.1016/j.jue.2005.03.005

Basker, E. (2005b). Job creation or destruction? Labor market effects of Wal-Mart expansion. *Review of Economics and Statistics, 87*(1), 174–183. https://doi.org/10.1162/0034653053327568

Bhagwati, J., & Panagariya, A. (2013). *Reforms and economic transformation in India*. Oxford University Press.

Bhasin, H. (2021). *Difference between organized and unorganized retailing*. Retrieved June 15, 2021. https://www.marketing91.com/organized-and-unorganized-retailing/

Child, P., Kilroy, T., & Naylor, J. (2015). *Modern grocery and the emerging-market consumer: A complicated courtship* (August). McKinsey & Company.

Gupta, S., & Ramachandran, D. (2021). Emerging market retail: Transitioning from a product-centric to a customer-centric approach. *Journal of Retailing, 97*(4), 597–620. https://doi.org/10.1016/j.jretai.2021.01.008

Jerath, K., Sajeesh, S., & Zhang, Z. J. (2016). A model of unorganized and organized retailing in emerging economies. *Marketing Science, 35*(5), 756–778. https://doi.org/10.1287/mksc.2015.0962

Jia, P. (2008). What happens when Wal-Mart comes to town: An empirical analysis of the discount retailing industry. *Econometrica, 76*(6), 1263–1316. https://doi.org/10.3982/ECTA6649

Kohli, R., & Bhagwati, J. (2011). Organized retailing in India: Issues and outlook [Columbia Business School Research paper]. *SSRN Electronic Journal, 12/25*. https://doi.org/10.2139/ssrn.2049901

Kumar, S. (2008). A study of the supermarket industry and its growing logistics capabilities. *International Journal of Retail and Distribution Management, 36*(3), 192–211. https://doi.org/10.1108/09590550810859150

Singh, V. P., Hansen, K. T., & Blattberg, R. C. (2006). Market entry and consumer behavior: An investigation of a Wal-Mart supercenter. *Marketing Science, 25*(5), 457–476. https://doi.org/10.1287/mksc.1050.0176

Sudhir, K., & Talukdar, D. (2015). The "Peter Pan syndrome" in emerging markets: The productivity-transparency trade-off in IT adoption. *Marketing Science, 34*(4), 500–521. https://doi.org/10.1287/mksc.2015.0921

Walters, D., & Knee, D. (1989). Competitive strategies in retailing. *Long Range Planning, 22*(6), 74–84. https://doi.org/10.1016/0024-6301(89)90104-0

PART II

Empirical Studies—Concepts and Implementations

CHAPTER 4

Customer Segmentation: SMPI Model

INTRODUCTION

The most critical challenges for organized retail players in the new landscape of increased competition are long-term growth and profitability. The unprecedented market dynamics force retailers to reconsider their business model and mode of operation. As a result of the rapid advancement of information technology, the entire world has become borderless. Thanks to the proliferation of retailing channels, customers now have more options and better service quality than ever. Many multinational retailers are planning to enter the fast-expanding retail sector in India, which is one of their top choices. Consumer mindset and purchasing patterns are rapidly changing due to technology and the internet (Khare, 2012). Even when making a small purchase, modern consumers evaluate their decision and the quality of the product they receive. Based on these comparisons, they post their reactions to their level of satisfaction on social media. Even offline consumers nowadays conduct online searches to obtain the necessary information and make a purchasing decision, attempting to immerse themselves in a completely different environment that will influence their purchasing habits. As a result, new consumer shopping behavior does not always follow the traditional pattern. Understanding consumers and their preferences are more important than ever in today's increasingly competitive retailing landscape to foster a high customer-centric approach. This indicates rapid

© The Author(s), under exclusive license to Springer Nature Singapore Pte Ltd. 2023
M. K. Dash et al., *Customer-Centricity in Organized Retailing*, https://doi.org/10.1007/978-981-19-3593-0_4

changes in retail consumers' purchasing patterns; thus, the preferences that lead consumers to decision-making play an essential role for retailers. Proper prediction of consumers' preferred factors and sub-factors can help retailers better serve the consumers according to their needs and wants and gain their positive reaction and attitude, thus, customer-centricity and loyalty.

Customer-centricity is a new and developing concept. In the last decade, customer-centricity has emerged as an emerging area of research, with many company reports on this specific concept being published and retailing research literature showing a gradual increase. With the rapid growth of technology and the high market dynamics in India, many companies are attempting to become more customer-centric to attract, align, and retain customers. Customer-centricity is a handy tool for increasing "Customer Lifetime Value (CLV)" by discovering new and unique ways to serve valuable customers. Customer-centricity is gaining traction among marketers all over the world. As a result, there is a strong need for research to find new consumer decision-making instruments (specifically, consumer preferences and shopping motivation) and, thus, a roadmap to customer-centricity in a dynamic retail market in the global scenario.

However, despite the emerging concept of customer-centricity gaining immense importance, current knowledge of customer-centricity is still limited; specifically, there is evidence of very little research on customer-centricity (no such research supported by empirical evidence) in the context of organized retailing, as well as limitations in current knowledge of how the roadmap for adopting and implementing customer-centricity works. The study's uniqueness lies in understanding organized retail consumers' purchasing behavior and preferences. This research aims to create a structural model of the pillars of customer-centricity in organized retailing. The empirical analysis meets the standard pre-model development stage requirements for developing the model. After developing and validating scales for all relevant constructs, the hypothetical model of consumer preference, shopping motivation, and patronage intention (SMPI Model) was proposed and tested using the structural equation modeling approach. The model's outcomes in terms of path estimates are listed and discussed. To understand the moderating effects of consumer demographics on the developed SMPI model of customer-centricity, the following sections of the chapter discuss the results of a moderating effect.

Segmentation of Organized Retail Store Shoppers

Because of the inextricable linkages between retail consumption patterns, preferences, and decision-making approaches, identifying retail customer behavior, preferences, and decision-making styles has attracted considerable attention from consumer behavioral practitioners and researchers over the years (Lysonski & Durvasula, 2013). However, while a significant conceptual and empirical study has been done on traditional consumer decision-making styles, very little has been explored on the Indian buying behavior and preferences dilemmas in organized retail. The first phase contextualizes the research problem by reviewing related literature on consumer behavior and preferences, shopping motivation (utilitarian and hedonic), patronage intention, customer-centricity, and decision-making science in organized retailing. Only a few research articles on customer-centricity have been published in academic journals. The authors who have studied customer-centricity and published their research articles in scholarly journals are—Homburg et al. (2000), Sheth et al. (2000), Shah et al. (2006), Shenoy et al. (2012), Lee et al. (2015), Hienerth et al. (2011), Lee et al. (2015), Sheth et al. (2011), Gebauer and Kowalkowski (2012), Lamberti (2013), and Christopher Hart (working paper) and Joseph Gagnon (magazine article) to name the most important and cited works. Even though the concept of customer-centricity is gaining traction like never before, almost all of the articles written and published on the subject are in the form of reports published by either corporate/business consulting houses or research-based organizations such as Technopak, Microsoft Corp., PWC, Peper & Rogers, KPMG, ATKearney, Booz-Allen Hamilton, IBM Business Consultancy. There are only a few hand-count published books on the much-discussed topic of the hour, namely, customer-centricity.

Sheth et al. (2000) explored the antecedents and consequences of customer-centric marketing. Mitreanu, C. has proposed a next-generation customer-centricity based on consumer expectations and the hierarchy of customer issues. Shah et al. (2006) suggest a customer-centric approach fueled by solid leadership commitment, organizational reconfiguration, technology and process support, and revised financial metrics. Gummersson, E. investigated "Customer centricity: reality or a wild goose chase?" to question the viability of customer-centricity and its axiom as the foundation for marketing and profitability. Lee et al.

(2015) empirically studied the impacts of structural sources of consumer-centric on firm performance. They concluded that customer-centric firms surpass their counterparts in strengthening customer-firm relationships, increasing customer value, and enhancing customer satisfaction. Customers should be at the core of any business model, and there should be an opportunity to win customers over at every touchpoint. Hienerth et al. (2011) reported in their research on user-centric business strategies' characteristics and implementation process. Integrating user-centric value propositions at established businesses is a challenging task requiring significant adjustments to conventional manufacturer-centered business strategies. Sheth et al. (2011) evaluated the customer-centric approach to sustainability and identified three main flaws: it does not explicitly emphasize the consumer. It fails to acknowledge the coming challenges from expanding global overconsumption. It does not take a holistic approach. Peppers and Rogers (2012) investigated customer-centricity versus customer experience. They discovered that the terms "customer-centricity" and "customer experience" are frequently treated as synonyms, with meanings similar to other terms such as "customer satisfaction," "customer focus," or "customer service." Gebauer and Kowalkowski (2012) explored customer-focused and service-focused perspectives in organizational structure to understand better the interdependence of consumer and service inclinations in the organizational structures of capital goods businesses. Lamberti (2013) studied customer-centricity: the construct and the operational antecedents. Michel et al. (2014) studied the development and validation of the Customer-Centered Behaviour (CCB) measure to develop and verify a new standard of customer service work performance through the Customer-Centered Behaviour (CCB) metric. Researchers like Michel et al. (2014), Lamberti (2013), Sheth et al. (2011), Lee et al. (2015), Hienerth et al. (2011), Shah et al. (2006), Sheth et al. (2000) and Homburg et al. (2000) in the field of marketing has also published conceptual works on customer-centricity and the scope, advantages, and challenges in adopting and practicing the same. However, the number of such literature is very few. Hardly any literature suggests the path to customer-centricity. However, some company reports have suggested conceptual roadmaps for adopting customer-centricity but badly lack empirical support. This study is motivated by a company report (Accenture Report, 2009). It empirically evaluates the proposed path model step-by-step to improve understanding of Customer-Centric Business Modeling (CCBM) in the Indian retail market.

Shenoy et al. (2012) conducted and reported a study on customer-centricity in India. According to Shenoy et al. (2012), customer-centric strategy methods supermarket retailers in India confront fierce competition from domestic and overseas competitors. The scholars suggest a theoretical framework for a customer-centric strategy that can help supermarkets acquire a competitive edge, but the competition among supermarkets in India is rising. As a result, developing an effective strategy to assist them in achieving superior performance has become critical. Undoubtedly, the emergence of new retail channels in India increases competition among retailers for a larger market share.

In this volatile market, a more focused approach is essential to build a new competitive advantage. One of the most prominent and influential ways to accomplish this is through a scientifically sound marketing and customer retention strategy. It is more expensive to acquire new customers than to keep existing ones. The evaluation of customer satisfaction, attitude, and intention has always been a matter of great interest for marketing and allied field scholars because a firm's capacity to obtain a competitive advantage over its competitors is dependent on how well it handles its marketing operations and relationships with customers (Wu et al., 2009). Several models were developed in the 1960s and 1970s to illustrate consumers' decision-making behavior and the most preferred factors influencing it. These models have remained the primary reference source even in the modern era. However, marketers are witnessing significant changes in consumer behavior, preferences, shopping motivation, and patronage intention as a result of the emergence of multiple retail channels and an adaptation of some different kinds of decision-making processes for the new environment (Xia & Sudharshan, 2002), the need for the development of new models for this specific context have recently been raised. This study aims to improve our understanding of organized retail consumer behavior by proposing a statistically validated model that describes the relationship between consumer preferences, shopping motivation (utilitarian and hedonic), and patronage intention.

Consumer preferences in India are changing as the country's standard of living rises. The demographic characteristics of consumers are strongly related to their purchasing behavior (Bhatnagar et al., 2000; Korgaonkar & Wolin, 1999). Demographic factors classify customers and better analyze each group's structure Demographics can influence store selection and visit behavior and purchase behavior (Mittal & Kamakura, 2001). On the other hand, these factors have rarely been investigated with a hypothesized consumer preference model and patronage intention to see if they have a moderating effect. This research examines the moderating impact of users' demographic features on the model of customer decision-making style in an online platform to fill a gap in the literature. However, little research has been conducted to date, particularly in the Indian context, to determine if customer preferences influence purchasing motivation and patronage intention (e.g., Rajagopal, 2011; Singh, 2015), which can be considered a baseline for retailers to be customer-centric by addressing consumer preferences issues through more efficient and targeted strategies. As a result, the purpose of this study is to establish an empirical link between the set of store attributes that organized retail store consumers prefer, their shopping motivations (utilitarian and hedonic) based on those preferential aspects, and their patronage intention. It is clear from this that scholars in retailing conceptually and empirically relate the concepts of utilitarian and hedonic shopping motives to different individual and distinct ideas, but not in a holistic consumer preference loom.

Various studies, such as those conducted by Jin and Kim (2003) and Westbrook and Black (1985), sought to investigate shoppers' motives as well as the link between these motivations and customers' behavior. Tauber (1972) distinguished two types of shopping motives: personal and social. These motives have a variety of characteristics. Personal motives involve role-playing, diversion, self-gratification, learning new trends, physical activity, and sensory stimulation. In contrast, social motives encompass social experiences outside the house, interaction with others who share the same interests, peer group attractions, status and authority, and bargaining happiness. Much research has indicated that shopping behavior can be related to utility motives such as task-related, product-oriented, and logical, and requires multi-faceted or hedonic motives like recreational, pleasurable, intrinsic, and stimulation-oriented motives. (e.g., Babin et al., 1994). This study examines the underlying influence of consumer preference attributes on utilitarian and hedonic shopping motives and, as a result, patronage intention. This study investigates the various utilitarian and hedonic factors influencing consumers' purchasing intentions for organized retail stores (supermarkets/hypermarkets). According to Dawson et al. (1990), the supermarket/hypermarket most likely caters to highly motivated consumers by hedonistic impulse. As a result, those customers are highly loyal to supermarkets/hypermarkets. These hedonic consumers are more concerned with the store's attributes (Arnold & Reynolds, 2003; Dawson et al., 1990). Though supermarkets/hypermarkets with high attributes likely stimulate shoppers' hedonic aspects, it is worth investigating whether shoppers with lower economic status and diversity may be motivated by utilitarian elements.

Pillars of Customer-Centricity

A moderation effect based on consumer attributes must be included to better understand customer-centricity in organized retail (Ranaweera et al., 2005). Demographics and other consumer attributes have been investigated in several scenarios to assess their moderating influence on purchase behavior (Bhatnagar et al., 2000; Korgaonkar & Wolin, 1999). These moderators represent the impact of customer differences, resulting in a more comprehensive understanding of consumer purchasing behavior and preferences in the context of organized retailing at the segment level rather than the less optimal aggregate level. This model should help marketing managers segment, and target organized retail customers while developing true customer-centricity and academics and researchers who want to learn more about this phenomenon (Bhatnagar et al., 2000). Customers' satisfaction and loyalty/patronage levels can be moderated by a set of unique characteristics of individuals, referred to here as customer characteristics (Bhatnagar et al., 2000; Ranaweera et al., 2005). These moderating effects on consumer behavior are more evident during the first transaction than in future transactions.

When reviewing the available literature on Indian retailing, it was discovered that several authors had discussed the generalizability of previously devised scales on consumer behavior, choice and preference (SERVPERF), service quality dimensions (SERVQUAL), and retail service quality (RSQS). On the other hand, consumer behavior and preferences differ significantly across cultures, and culture shifts across geographical boundaries. According to the available literature, retail scholars discuss service quality (Parasuraman et al., 1988), retail service quality (Dabholkar, 1995), store choice attributes (Leszczyc et al., 2000), loyalty parameters (Kuruvilla & Joshi, 2010; Zhang & Breugelmans, 2012), and antecedents of consumer satisfaction (Sirgy et al., 2000; Voss et al., 2003). Some researchers have looked into retail consumer preferences, but not with a comprehensive view of organized retailing. Scholars who have studied consumer preferences in the Indian organized retail setting have primarily used factor/attribute-based analysis or have focused solely on individual factors such as store atmospherics, ambiance, assortment, pricing, and entertainment. The literature lacks in developing and validating a holistic, contemporary consumer preference scale in the Indian organized retail context. This study is motivated to fill this gap by developing and validating the factor structure of the consumer preference scale in the context of Indian organized retailing. Furthermore, the study assesses the impact of demographics on the Shopping Motivation and Patronage Intention (SMPI) Model in Organized Retailing based on Consumer Preference and Customer-Centricity dimensions.

The empirical analysis is carried out in three stages to achieve the research objectives: (a) Scale Development, (b) Scale Validation (c) Structural Model of Pillars of Customer-Centricity. Accordingly, the methodology followed for completing this research work is segregated into three parts: (i) Methodology for scale development, (ii) Methodology for scale validation, and (iii) Methodology for the formulation of the structural model. Each methodological part is explained in detail first, and then the entire empirical analysis is carried out concerning the methodology explained. Table 4.1 depicts the data procedure and the outline of the entire methodological process used in this chapter.

Phase-1: The first phase summarizes the research problem by reviewing relevant literature on consumer behavior and preferences., their shopping motivation (utilitarian and hedonic) and patronage intention, customer-centricity, and decision-making science in the context of organized retailing. The literature review is a crucial component of every study to identify gaps. After identifying the variables of consumer behavior and preferences, their shopping motivation (utilitarian and hedonic) and patronage intention from literature, to undertake exploratory research, an in-depth interview and focus group study was conducted to refine all factors (related to the said issues) in the context of organized retailing. After variables identification, a pilot questionnaire was prepared for the pilot testing. The final questionnaire was designed to be brief, neat, and attractive, addressing the objectives and obtaining accurate data. Data was collected through direct interaction and a self-administered survey method. A self-administered questionnaire containing the various consumer shopping behavior, purchase intention, and attributes preferences were prepared. In addition to the background demographics

Table 4.1 Research procedure followed

Stage 1 Objective 1	Scale Development and Scale Validation	Step 1	Citation Analysis of Factors and Variables	
		Step 2	Exploratory Research	In-Depth Interview
				Focus Group
		Step 3	Pilot Questionnaire	
		Step 4	Pilot Testing	
		Step 5	Final Questionnaire Design	
		Step 6	Data Collection	
		Step 7	Item Analysis and Scale Refinement (Validity and Reliability Check)	
		Step 8	Exploratory Factor Analysis (EFA)	Consumers' Most Preferred Store Attributes
				Consumer Shopping Motivation and Patronage Intention
		Reliability, Validity		Cronbach α, KMO
		Step 9	Confirmatory Factor Analysis (CFA)	Consumers' Most Preferred Store Attributes
				Consumer Shopping Motivation and Patronage Intention
		Step 10	Validation	Face Validity
				Convergent Validity
				Discriminant Validity
				Nomonological Validity

(continued)

Table 4.1 (continued)

Stage 2 Objective 2	*Structural Model*	Step 1	Structural Model of Pillars of Customer-Centricity in Organized Retailing (SEM)	
		Step 2	Moderating Effect of Demographic Characteristics	Gender
				Age
				Education Level
				Occupation
				Marital Status
				Income

(Section A), the survey tool has Three (03) more sections. Section "B" of the questionnaire contains only close-ended questions to explore consumers' general shopping behavior, likeness, intention, and preferences. Section "C" determines how essential items/variables are to the respondents/customers using a five-point Likert scale of 69 items. Section "D" is composed of a series of items describing the hedonic and utilitarian attitude of the customer/respondents. This section is used in the questionnaire to determine whether mall consumers in India have "Hedonic" or 'Utilitarian' attitudes and establish a link between hedonic and utilitarian shopping motivation and customers' most preferred super/hypermarket store attributes. Section D' incorporates questions to discover what the customer basket contains and the factors that influence the customer basket. During this survey phase, all the store managers were also approached with a structured questionnaire for general store-related information such as footfall and conversion rate. The study's scope is restricted to seven major cities in India, as primary data gathering is limited to organized retail chains operating in Seven (07) significant cities in India in different geographical parts of the country state, namely *Delhi, Mumbai, Kolkatta, Bangalore, Hyderabad, Chennai, and Bhubaneswar* the categories General Merchandise, Apparel & Accessories (*G.M. & A*) are taken into account. Retail chains exclusively dealing with jewelry, white consumer goods (electronics and home appliances), fruits and vegetables, and grocery items are excluded from the study.

Phase 2: Exploratory Factor Analysis (EFA) with Principal Component Analysis using varimax rotation identifies the factor structure. The methodology for scale development is only performed for the scale intended to develop consumers' preferred attributes with 69 items. For the other two constructs (i.e., consumer shopping motivation and patronage intention), the same methodology is followed even if the items for these two constructs are taken directly from previously tested scales by researchers (still, the item analysis output is furnished for justification). All the constructs were subjected to exploratory factor analysis to justify the scales' reliability and validity in the current study context.

The original collection of variables must be transformed into a new set of uncorrelated variables to derive the factor structure of consumers' preferred qualities, purchasing motivations, and patronage intention in the organized retail context. PCA reduces a larger group of variables into more minor variables that reflect the essential dimensions of variability and summarizes observed variability using a smaller number of components

(Bhattacharyya et al., 2023; Field, 2000; Hair et al., 2010). Generally, 300 cases are probably adequate, but commonalities after extraction should probably be above 0.50 (Field, 2000; Hair et al., 2010), but data collected from 682 respondents are used in this study. Therefore, the sample size is not a problem for analysis. After scale refinement, forty variables/items were left for further research. The next threat to valid inferences of PCA is the Kaiser–Meyer–Olkin (KMO) measure of sampling adequacy. Bartlett's test of sphericity means factorability, i.e., the appropriateness of PCA (Field, 2000). For the data, the KMO value is 0.834 (for the consumer preference construct) and 0.782 (for shopping motivation and patronage intention constructs)—both are in a suitable category (Field, 2000). Bartlett's test is highly significant for both cases ($p < 0.001$). The Total Variance explained 51.683 and 50.048%, respectively, for both the constructs), the eigenvalues associated with each factor extracted linear components) after the rotated component matrix is furnished in Tables 4.2 and 4.3 (Field, 2000). Another eight variables were eliminated from the consumer preference scale (29 items were eliminated in the scale refinement stage). No elimination was done for the consumer shopping motivation and intention construct (one item was eliminated during scale refinement). A rotated component matrix was obtained of the factor loadings for each variable into each factor. The Varimax rotation method was used in this study to rotate elements. The component matrix showed that all the indicator items loaded above 0.45 (Hair et al., 1998) on their respective factors and below 0.40 on all the other factors (see Tables 4.4 and 4.7) for both the constructs, which is said to be fair (Comrey & Lee, 1992). However, only a few loading are slightly lower but not less than 0.41 in both "consumer preference" and "shopping motivation and patronage intention" constructs. As the sample size for this study is quite large 682), the factor loadings above 0.30 are even practically significant (Hair et al., 1998). After identifying all factors, the reliability of each element and its underlying variables was determined using Cronbach's alpha concepts.

The data is used in an Exploratory Factor Analysis (EFA) to determine the underlying structure. EFA frequently employs orthogonal rotation and cross-loadings as long as they are kept to a minimum. Confirmatory Factor Analysis (CFA) specifies the factor structure based on a "good" theory. The CFA is then used to see if the proposed theoretical factor structure has any empirical support.

After identifying nine factors for *consumers' preferred attributes* in organized retailing, their *shopping motive* (utilitarian and hedonic), and *patronage intention* through PCA, the next stage is to confirm the factor structure and provide a procedure for testing unidimensionality (Hair et al., 2010) through CFA. In the first step to getting the model to fit well, those variables had a low factor loading of less than 0.50, and a correlation value of less than 0.40 was checked in the Table of variables of CFA (Hair et al., 2010; Kline, 2011). Tables 4.2 and 4.3 show that the factor loading of each variable to their respective factor >0.60 and squared multiple correlations approximately >0.40 (Tables 4.4 and 4.5) indicates the acceptable level. However, based on factor loading and squared multiple correlations, confirmation of the entire model cannot be stated without assessing goodness-of-fit indices and measurement model validity. *Goodness-of-Fit (GOF)* indicates (see Tables 4.10 and 4.11) how well the specified model reproduces the covariance matrix among the indicator (Hair et al., 2010). Researchers have focused on improving and developing measures representing various aspects of the model's ability to represent data since the initial GOF measure was developed (Kline, 2011).

Structural Equation Models represent the relationship among the latent variables of interest and models describing the link between them and their manifest or observable indicators (Bhattacharyya et al., 2023). Structural Equation Modeling (SEM) is a statistical approach that allows for complicated interactions between independent and dependent variables. Structural Equation Modeling differs from Confirmatory Factor Analysis (CFA). CFA is a measurement model and a visual representation that describes the model's components, indicator variables, and interrelations. The Structural equation model (SEM) is a set of dependent relationships connecting the hypothesized model's constructs, whereas the CFA gives quantitative evaluations of the constructs' validity and reliability. SEM examines if the variables are related and, in conjunction with CFA, allows the researcher to accept or reject the proposed hypothesis. The baseline model is also used to assess (Hypotheses 1–20).

The baseline model tests the hypotheses regarding consumers' preferred attributes and utilitarian shopping motive (Hypotheses 1–9), consumers' preferred attributes in the organized retailing environment, and hedonic shopping motive (Hypotheses 10–18); then, between consumers' shopping motive (utilitarian and hedonic) and patronage intention (Hypotheses 19 and 20). After establishing the model, it was tested whether the consumers' demographic characteristics moderate the model (Hypotheses 21-26). Further, it is also investigated whether the demographic characteristics of shoppers have any moderating effect on the structural relationships. Finally, an overview is presented to highlight the main findings.

Empirical Analysis

All the empirical analyses performed are presented in this section. The empirical analysis performed is divided into three parts as follows. (i) Identification of consumers' preferred attributes in organized retail set-up and their shopping motives and patronage intention, (ii) Validation of the identified features of Consumer preferences, Shopping motive and patronage intention, (iii) Structural model of pillars of customer-centricity in organized retailing and moderating effect of consumers' demographic characteristics.

Identification of Factor Constructs for Consumer Preference, Shopping Motives, and Patronage Intention in Organized Retailing

Exploratory factor analysis (EFA) was used to identify the factors/attributes consumers prefer in organized retail settings and their shopping motives and patronage intention. EFA was performed separately using SPSS 20.0 for both scales, i.e., for consumer preferences and shopping motivation and patronage intention using the methodology described previously. Results for both scales are furnished separately in Tables 4.2 and 4.3. In the factor extraction stage, various statistical rules were taken into account. As finalized in the item discrimination stage, the two sets of test variables, 40 and 14, were subjected to principal component analysis using SPSS 20.0. Before performing the analysis, the suitability of data was thoroughly assessed as illustrated in the methodology section, with a KMO value of 0.834 and 0.782 and Bartlett's Test of Sphericity reaching statistical significance ($p < 0.001$) for both sets of variables, the data was deemed to be fit for further analysis. Eigenvalues were used to determine the number of extracted factors.

After receiving the SPSS output, the item reliabilities, communalities, factor loadings, and percentage of variance explained by each identified factor were checked, and Cronbach's alpha. Both scales were finalized after obtaining satisfactory scores per the rule of thumb for the said measures. Nine factors for the consumer preference scale and three scales for consumers' shopping motivation (utilitarian and hedonic) and patronage intention were extracted. The Total Variance explained by nine extracted components for the consumer preference scale was 51.683%, and for the consumer motive and patronage intention scale, it was 50.048%. Consumers' preference for super/hypermarket stores' attributes is 51.683%, explained by the identified nine factors and its underlying 32 variables. The rest may lie on some other preferences that could not be covered in the specified scale. Similarly, the three components with 14 variables in the consumer shopping motivation and patronage intention scale account for 50.048% of variations in total The rest may be caused by some other factors/instincts that are not explored in this study (see Tables 4.2 and 4.3).

The nine constructs for the consumer preference scale and three constructs for the consumer motivation and intention scale are solely selected based on eigenvalue criteria >1. First, nine components were identified (Table 4.2) and named logically in the consumer preference scale. The first and foremost factor of consumer preference in the context of organized retail super/hypermarket store environment includes four variables/statements: Ambience of shopping mall attractive storefront and display window, exterior color, lighting, hoardings, and décor (S66, Loading—0.655), Aesthetics of shopping mall Interior lighting, décor, Air Condition, Music and Fragrance (S68, Loading—0.646), Clean enough and well mopped washed exterior and interior (S67, Loading—0.638) and High-quality store facilities (drinking water, separate clean gents and ladies toilets, lift/escalator, seating area inside store couch/sofa and outside store canopy) (S65, Loading—0.560), so the factor is named as *"Store Atmospherics"* which explains 16.786% of the total variance and hence termed as the topmost preferred attribute by shoppers. The second extracted component includes four variables/ statements: Value for money for every purchase (S15, Loading—0.642), Discounts/special offers on occasions (S14, Loading—0.605), Affordable price range of products (S21, Loading—0.430) and loyalty rewards as cash discount/special offers for regular customers (S40, Loading—0.417), so it is named as *"Pricing and Value"* which explains 5.602% of the total variance. The third extracted component includes three variables: Availability of never stock out wide variety Deep (assortment) (S23, Loading—0.689), Availability of latest and trendy product range (S22,

Table 4.2 Identified consumers' preferred attributes/factors in organized retailing

Factors	Variables/Items	Mean	Reliability	Communalities	Factor loadings	Eigen value	% of Variance explained
Store Atmospherics	Ambience (S66)	3.85	0.820	0.562	0.655	5.238	16.786
	Aesthetics (S68)	4.04	0.824	0.556	0.646		
	Cleanliness (S67)	4.02	0.822	0.582	0.638		
	Store Facilities (S65)	3.90	0.817	0.527	0.560		
Pricing and Value (F2)	Value for Money (S15)	3.85	0.820	0.530	0.642	1.665	5.602
	Discount/Special offer (S14)	4.06	0.822	0.482	0.605		
	Affordability (S21)	3.73	0.820	0.479	0.430		
	Loyalty cash discount/offers (S40)	3.90	0.820	0.500	0.417		
Assortment (F3)	Never stock-out wide variety (S23)	3.80	0.823	0.532	0.689	1.451	4.935
	Latest and trendy products (S22)	3.81	0.819	0.547	0.615		
	Attractive product display and placement (S10)	3.88	0.821	0.504	0.428		
In-store Delights (F4)	Touch and feel/In-store trail (S33)	3.85	0.824	0.491	0.637	1.371	4.685

Factors	Variables/Items	Mean	Reliability	Communalities	Factor loadings	Eigen value	% of Variance explained
	Fast and easy billing/POS/Checkout (S17)	3.83	0.821	0.481	0.607		
	In-store digitization (S32)	3.84	0.821	0.522	0.559		
	Customer consultancy (S26)	3.82	0.819	0.481	0.500		
Convenience (F5)	One stop shopping (S3)	4.09	0.822	0.543	0.722	1.308	4.489
	Large and spacious store with proper signage (S4)	4.10	0.822	0.487	0.610		
	Location (S5)	3.76	0.821	0.465	0.564		
Product/Service Quality and Reliability (F6)	High-quality branded product (S44)	3.90	0.821	0.591	0.703	1.233	3.955
	Reliable and high-quality services (S13)	3.83	0.823	0.451	0.594		
	Reliable information sharing (S46)	3.88	0.816	0.467	0.473		

(continued)

Table 4.2 (continued)

Factors	Variables/Items	Mean	Reliability	Communalities	Factor loadings	Eigen value	% of Variance explained
Person-to-Person Experience (F7)	Highly responsive prompt service (S28)	3.52	0.826	0.458	0.724	1.162	3.831
	Empathy/politeness in behavior (S42)	3.78	0.822	0.486	0.489		
	Highly informative staff with good knowledge on offerings (S19)	3.50	0.828	0.542	0.439		
	Individual customer attention (S47)	3.84	0.818	0.595	0.414		
Problem-Solving (F8)	Prompt handling of customer complaint and queries (S54)	3.95	0.824	0.482	0.638	1.142	3.768
	Consideration of customer feedback/VOC for service improvement (S25)	3.82	0.819	0.478	0.586		
	Hassle free exchange/return policy (S11)	3.81	0.821	0.521	0.437		

Factors	Variables/Items	Mean	Reliability	Communalities	Factor loadings	Eigen value	% of Variance explained
Entertainment F(9)	Guarantee/Warranty (S35)	3.70	0.820	0.509	0.414	1.072	3.650
	Recreation/hang out (S1)	4.41	0.825	0.555	0.599		
	Food zones (S2)	4.17	0.824	0.507	0.531		
	Movies/shows (S12)	4.16	0.825	0.529	0.526		
				Total Variance Explained			51.683

Cronbach's Alpha: 0.826, KMO: 0.834, Bartlett's test of Sphericity (Chi-Square): 3199.454, Significance: 0.000, df: 496, $n = 682$ (32 Variables/Items)

Items S7, S18, S20, S39, S43, S45, S49, and S57 were eliminated from the 40 items selected in the item discrimination stage

Source Estimated from Primary Data

Loading—0.615), and Attractive display and proper placement of products in super/hypermarket stores (S10, Loading—0.428) thus named as *"Assortment"* which accounts for 4.935% of the total variance. The fourth construct explained 4.685% of the total variance named *"In-store Delights"* includes four variables: Touch and feel and opportunity to the in-store trial of products (S33, Loading—0.637), Hassle-free and less time-consuming Point of Sales (POS)/Billing (S17, Loading—0.607), In-store digitization Digital information sharing (through big digital screens, audiovisual aids, smartphone app, Wi-Fi and NFC Near Field Communication) (S32, Loading—0.559) and Service facilitators like gift consultant and fashion/style guides (S26, Loading—0.500). The fifth factor explained 4.489% of the total variance. They included three variables: Availability of all stuff under one roof, i.e., One-Stop Shopping (S3, Loading—0.722), a Shopping mall with a large floor area with proper signage (S4, Loading—0.610), and Malls situated in prime market location of the city (area of high retail concentration) (S5, Loading—0.564), thus named as *"Convenience."* The sixth factor includes three items: Availability of high-quality branded products (S44, Loading—0.703), Reliable and high-quality services provided by shopping malls/centers (S13, Loading—0.594), and Reliable information sharing by shopping malls on the latest offerings (product and services) (S46, Loading—0.473) and named as "Product/Service Quality & Reliability" which explained 3.955% of the total variance. The seventh construct explained 3.831% of the variance comprised of four attributes: High responsiveness and service promptness of shopping mall staff (S28, Loading—0.724), Mall employees' willingness to help, by heart treatment, and politeness (S42, Loading—0.489), Mall employees' product knowledge and ability to provide relevant information on all offerings (Product and Services) (S19, Loading—0.439) and Mall employees' customer attention and response to customer's queries (S47, Loading—0.414) thus named as *"Person-to-Person Experience."* The eighth factor explained 3.768% of variance incorporates four variables: Listening to customer queries and efficient complaint handling (S54, Loading—0.638), Listening to customers' feedback, suggestions, and voice of the customer (VOC) (S25, Loading—0.586), Easy, hassle-free return/exchange policy (S11, Loading—0.437) and Guarantee/Warranty and complete assurance for product purchased (S35, Loading—0.414) and hence named as *"Problem-Solving."* The ninth and last factor accounts for 3.650% of the total variance. It includes three variables: Good place for recreation, social connectivity, and hanging out with friends/family (S1, Loading—0.599), Food zone inside shopping mall/mall premises (S2, Loading—0.531), and Fun time and enjoyment by way of movies/events/fashion shows at large shopping centers (S12, Loading—0.526) named as '*Entertainment.*'

From the above illustration, it is noticeable that the top five consumer-preferred attributes among all extracted construct are: *highly responsive prompt service, one-stop shopping, high quality branded products, never stock-out wide variety deep assortment)* and *ambiance* in the context of a super/hypermarket store environment.

The constructs re-extracted for the shopping motivation (adopted from Voss et al., 2003) are two in number (refers to Table 4.3). Adding the patronage intention scale (adopted from Taylor & Todd, 1995) comes in three numbers. Among the two constructs about shopping motivation, the first construct explained 23.192% of the total variance comprised of five items: Visiting a shopping mall is useful (Functional) (A3, Loading—0.797), Visiting a shopping mall is a practical idea to fulfill a need (A5, Loading—0.740), Visiting a shopping mall is a practical (valuable) experience (A1, Loading—0.658), Mall shopping is helpful to meet my needs (A2, Loading—0.642) and I feel shopping in shopping mall as a necessary activity for me (A4, Loading—0.632) thus named as "*Utilitarian Motive*" (Voss et al., 2003). The second construct explained 12.194% of the variance and incorporated four items: Visiting a shopping mall is a delightful experience (A8, Loading—0.701), Visiting a shopping mall is a thrilling experience (A9, Loading—0.598), Visiting a shopping mall is an exciting experience (A7, Loading—0.595) and Visiting a shopping mall is an enjoyable experience (A10, Loading—0.494) hence named as "*Hedonic Motive*" (Voss et al., 2003). The other construct explained 14.662% of variance comprised of five variables: Chance of remaining loyal to the shopping mall (Keep on repeatedly purchasing from the same mall) (Int4, Loading—0.726), Likeliness to tell/refer others (Int5, Loading—0.721), intention to purchase (products) from this mall in my next visit (Int3, Loading—0.605), Likeliness of buying something from this mall whenever I visit (Int1, Loading—0.464) and Likeliness to pay some extra money for customizes product/service as per my wish (Int2, Loading—0.421) hence termed as '*Patronage Intention*' (Taylor & Todd, 1995).

Table 4.3 Re-identified constructs for consumers' shopping motivation and patronage intention in organized retailing

Factors	Variables	Mean	Reliability	Communalities	Factor loadings	Eigen value	% of Variance explained
Utilitarian Motive	Visiting to shopping mall is useful Functional (A3)	3.35	0.702	0.450	0.797	3.102	23.192
	Visiting a shopping mall is a practical idea to fulfill a need (A5)	3.45	0.707	0.428	0.740		
	Visiting shopping mall is an effective (valuable) experience (A1)	2.71	0.709	0.652	0.658		
	Mall shopping is helpful to meet my needs (A2)	3.42	0.711	0.502	0.642		
	I feel shopping in a shopping mall a necessary activity for me (A4)	3.79	0.718	0.564	0.632		
Hedonic Motive	Visiting shopping mall is a delightful experience (A8)	3.95	0.725	0.566	0.701	1.287	12.194
	Visiting shopping mall is a thrilling experience (A9)	3.98	0.718	0.491	0.598		

Factors	Variables	Mean	Reliability	Communalities	Factor loadings	Eigen value	% of Variance explained
	Visiting shopping mall is an exciting experience (A7)	3.54	0.722	0.578	0.595		
	Visiting a shopping mall is an enjoyable experience (A10)	3.32	0.716	0.494	0.586		
Patronage Intention	Chance of remaining loyal to the shopping mall (Keep on repeatedly purchasing from the same mall) (Int4)	3.32	0.709	0.503	0.726	1.773	14.662
	Likeliness to tell/refer others (Int5)	3.42	0.718	0.475	0.721		
	Intention to purchase (products) from this mall in my next visit (Int3)	3.59	0.723	0.570	0.605		
	The Likeliness of buying something from this mall whenever I visit (Int1)	3.72	0.715	0.547	0.464		

(continued)

Table 4.3 (continued)

Factors	Variables	Mean	Reliability	Communalities	Factor loadings	Eigen value	% of Variance explained
	Likeliness to pay some extra money for customize product/service as per my wish (Int2)	3.22	0.720	0.547	0.421		
	Total Variance Explained						50.048

Cronbach's Alpha: 0.730, KMO: 0.782, Bartlett's Test of Sphericity (Chi-Square): 1395.614, Significance: 0.000, df: 91, $n = 682$
Item A6 was eliminated from the Shopping Motivation scale adopted from Voss et al. (2003), and no item was eliminated from the Patronage Intention scale adopted from Taylor and Todd (1995)
Source Estimated from Primary Data

Validation of the Identified Factors for Consumer Preferences, Shopping Motivation and Patronage Intention

After identifying factors, the net task was to validate the factor structures. Confirmatory Factor Analysis (CFA) using AMOS 20.0 validated the identified factor structures in EFA. This section validated the facture structure, and the reliability and validity indices were examined using the rules described in the methodology section (Tables 4.4, 4.5, 4.6, 4.7, 4.8 and 4.9).

Assessing the Model Fit for Consumer Preference Scale and Consumer Shopping Motivation and Patronage Intention Scale

Several recommended tests, as described in the methodology part, were used to assess model adequacy, including the chi-square value normalized by degrees of freedom (CMIN/df), the root means square error of approximation (RMSEA), and the comparative fit index (CFI) (Byrne, 2001; Hu & Bentler, 1999), GFI, AGFI and NFI. Table 4.5 depicts all the requisite model fit indices for the consumer preference scale with recommended acceptance levels and how far the test results meet the recommendations in a separate remark column. The CFA results summarized in Table 4.5 for the consumer preference scale and Table 4.8 for the consumer shopping motivation and patronage intention scale demonstrate that model fit indices fulfill the recommended criteria, indicating that all constructs in both scales are unidimensional (Hu & Bentler, 1999).

As mentioned in the methodology section, factor loading and composite reliability (C.R.) was utilized to assess the dependability of the items within each factor. As shown in Tables 4.4 and 4.7, the factor loading standardized regression coefficient) of all items exceeds the recommended level of 0.60 (Bagozzi & Yi, 1988; Hair et al., 2010; Kline, 2011) in both the scales and composite reliability (C.R.) calculated as per (Eqn. 12) of all the constructs in both scales (Tables 4.4 and 4.7) exceed the widely accepted rule of thumb of 0.70, indicating appropriate measuring scale reliability (Fornell & Bookstein, 1982; Fornell & Larcker, 1981; Hair et al., 2010; Kline, 2011; Nunnally, 1978).

To assess the convergent validity of the scales, average variance extracted (AVE) was calculated following Eqn. 13, and comparisons were made with composite reliabilities obtained. As methodology suggests,

Table 4.4 Reliability of identified factors for consumer preference scale

Factors	Sub-factor	Coding	Loading	Item reliabilities	Delta	AVE	CR
F1 Store Atmospherics (SA)	Ambience	S65	0.770	0.593	0.407	0.5012	0.800345
	Aesthetics	S67	0.698	0.487	0.513		
	Cleanliness	S68	0.682	0.465	0.535		
	Store Facilities	S66	0.678	0.460	0.540		
F2 Pricing and Value (PV)	Value for Money	S40	0.746	0.557	0.443	0.4711	0.780288
	Discount and Special Offers	S21	0.683	0.466	0.534		
	Affordability	S14	0.676	0.457	0.543		
	Loyalty Cash discount/Special Offers	S15	0.636	0.404	0.596		
F3 Assortment (AST)	Deep Assortment (Availability of never stock out wide variety)	S10	0.684	0.468	0.532	0.4894	0.740933
	Latest and Trendy Products	S22	0.767	0.588	0.412		
	Attractive Product Display and Placement	S23	0.642	0.412	0.588		
F4 In-Store Delights (ISD)	Touch and Feel/In-store Trail	S26	0.789	0.623	0.377	0.4856	0.789512
	Fast and easy Billing/POS/Checkout	S32	0.691	0.477	0.523		

Factors	Sub-factor	Coding	Loading	Item reliabilities	Delta	AVE	CR
	In-store Digitization (Digital information Sharing)	S17	0.657	0.432	0.568		
	Customer Consultancy	S33	0.641	0.411	0.589		
F5 Convenience (CNV)	One Stop Shopping	S5	0.745	0.555	0.445	0.4538	0.712477
	Large Spacious Store with Signage	S4	0.637	0.406	0.594		
	Prime Location	S3	0.633	0.401	0.599		
F6 Product/Service Quality and Reliability (PSQR)	High Quality Branded Products	S46	0.779	0.607	0.393	0.5097	0.756388
	Reliable and High Quality Service	S13	0.668	0.446	0.554		
	Reliable Information Sharing (on latest offerings)	S44	0.690	0.476	0.524		
F7 Person to Person Experience (PPE)	Highly responsive Prompt Service	S47	0.736	0.542	0.458	0.4649	0.776118
	Empathy/Politeness in Behaviour	S19	0.651	0.424	0.576		

(continued)

Table 4.4 (continued)

Factors	Sub-factor	Coding	Loading	Item reliabilities	Delta	AVE	CR
	Highly Informative staff with Good Knowledge on Offerings (Product and Services)	S42	0.680	0.462	0.538		
	Individual Customer Attention	S28	0.657	0.432	0.568		
F8 Problem Solving (PS)	Prompt handling of Customer Complaint and Queries	S35	0.773	0.598	0.402	0.4836	0.788487
	Listening to VOC	S11	0.665	0.442	0.558		
	Hassle Free Exchange/Return Policy	S25	0.688	0.473	0.527		
	Guarantee/Warrantee	S54	0.649	0.421	0.579		
F9 Entertainment (ENT)	Recreation/Hang Out	S12	0.713	0.508	0.492	0.4516	0.711456
	Food Court	S2	0.662	0.438	0.562		
	Movie/Shows	S1	0.639	0.408	0.592		

Source Estimated from Primary Data

Table 4.5 Discriminant validity of consumer preference scale (AVE and squared inter-construct correlations—SIC Comparison)

| | AVE | CR | Squared Inter-construct Correlations (SIC) ||||||||
			SA	PV (F2)	AST (F3)	ISD (F4)	CNV (F5)	PSQR (F6)	PPE (F7)	PS (F8)	ENT (F9)
SA	0.5012	0.800345	0.7079*								
PV (F2)	0.4711	0.780288	0.442225	0.6863*							
AST (F3)	0.4894	0.740933	0.184041	0.421201	0.6995*						
ISD (F4)	0.4856	0.789512	0.248004	0.355216	0.443556	0.6968*					
CNV (F5)	0.4538	0.712477	0.228484	0.3249	0.271441	0.187489	0.6736*				
PSQR(F6)	0.5097	0.756388	0.3364	0.408321	0.268324	0.301401	0.237169	0.7139*			
PPE (F7)	0.4649	0.776118	0.331776	0.450241	0.357604	0.252004	0.213444	0.374544	0.6818*		
PS (F8)	0.4836	0.788487	0.337561	0.431649	0.383161	0.4489	0.299209	0.400689	0.405769	0.6954*	
ENT (F9)	0.4516	0.711456	0.184041	0.181476	0.318096	0.218089	0.349281	0.266256	0.162409	0.198025	0.6720*

*Replaced with square roots of the Average Variance Extracted (AVE)—all values greater than off-diagonal elements in the corresponding rows and columns and exceeds the correlations between a given construct

Source Estimated from Primary Data

Table 4.6 Reliability of re-identified factor structure for consumer shopping motivation and patronage intention

	Sub-factor	Loading	Item reliabilities	Delta	AVE	CR
Utilitarian Motive	Visiting to shopping mall is useful (Functional) (A3)	0.605	0.366	0.634	0.5113014	0.837368
	Visiting a shopping mall is a practical idea to fulfill a need (A5)	0.654	0.428	0.572		
	Visiting shopping mall is an effective (valuable) experience (A1)	0.673	0.453	0.547		
	Mall shopping is helpful to meet my needs (A2)	0.754	0.569	0.431		
	I feel shopping in a shopping mall a necessary activity for me (A4)	0.861	0.741	0.259		
Hedonic Motive	Visiting shopping mall is an enjoyable experience (A10)	0.783	0.613	0.387	0.5042263	0.802093
	Visiting a shopping mall is an exciting experience (A7)	0.674	0.454	0.546		
	Visiting a shopping mall is a thrilling experience (A9)	0.696	0.484	0.516		
	Visiting shopping mall is a delightful experience (A8)	0.682	0.465	0.535		
Patronage Intention	Chance of remaining loyal to the shopping mall (Keep on repeatedly purchasing from the same mall) (Int4)	0.593	0.352	0.648	0.5082762	0.836063
	Likeliness to tell/refer others (Int5)	0.745	0.555	0.445		

Sub-factor	Loading	Item reliabilities	Delta	AVE	CR
Intention to purchase (products) from this mall in my next visit (Int3)	0.633	0.401	0.599		
Likeliness of buying something from this mall whenever I visit (Int1)	0.757	0.573	0.427		
Likeliness to pay some extra money for customizes product/service as per my wish (Int2)	0.813	0.661	0.339		

Source Estimated from Primary Data

Table 4.7 Goodness-of-fit results of shopping motivation and patronage intention measurement model

Fit measure	Goodness fit index (measurement model)	Remarks
x^2/df (CMIN/df)	2.122	Good Fit
RMSEA	0.041	Good Fit
p Value for Test of Close Fit (RMSEA < 0.05)	0.961	Good Fit
NFI	0.888	Acceptable Fit
CFI	0.937	Acceptable Fit
GFI	0.967	Acceptable Fit
AGFI	0.954	Acceptable Fit

Source Estimated from Primary Data

Table 4.8 Discriminant validity for shopping motivation and patronage intention (AVE and squared interconstruct correlations—SIC comparison)

	AVE	CR	Squared Interconstruct Correlations (SIC)		
			Utilitarian Motive	Hedonic Motive	Patronage Intention
Utilitarian Motive	0.5113	0.837368	0.7150*		
Hedonic Motive	0.5042	0.802093	0.173056	0.7100*	
Patronage Intention	0.5082	0.836063	0.209764	0.295936	0.7128*

*Replaced with square roots of the Average Variance Extracted (AVE)—all values greater than off-diagonal elements in the corresponding rows and columns and exceeds the correlations between a given construct

AVE values were less than C.R. values in all the scales' cases. An AVE of 0.50 or higher is a good rule of thumb, offering adequate convergence and that the scale has higher distinct validity (Fornell & Larcker, 1981), but C.R. must be greater than AVE (Hair et al., 2010). However, (Malhotra & Dash, 2011, p. 702) notes that "AVE is a more conservative measure than C.R. Based on C.R. alone, the researcher may conclude that the convergent validity of the construct is adequate, even though more than 50% of the variance is due to error." As shown in Tables 4.6 and 4.9, average variance extracted (AVE) values ranging from 0.4516 to 0.5097 and 0.5042 to 0.5113, respectively, in both scales, are approximately close to or above 0.50 in all cases. Less than C.R. values in all cases indicated that each construct is highly related to its respective indicators (Malhotra & Dash, 2011). Hence, convergent validity is adequate in both scales.

Table 4.9 Path estimates for SMPI model of customer-centricity

			Estimate (β)	S.E.	C.R.	p
Store Atmospherics	→	Utilitarian Motive	0.235	0.082	2.854	0.004**
Pricing and Value	→	Utilitarian Motive	−0.058	0.124	−0.467	0.641
Assortment	→	Utilitarian Motive	0.017	0.128	0.136	0.892
In-Store Delights	→	Utilitarian Motive	−0.002	0.096	−0.025	0.98
Convenience	→	Utilitarian Motive	0.176	0.108	1.632	0.103
Product/Service Quality and Reliability	→	Utilitarian Motive	0.092	0.093	0.985	0.324
Person-to-Person Experience	→	Utilitarian Motive	−0.039	0.122	−0.317	0.751
Problem-Solving	→	Utilitarian Motive	0.776	0.189	4.114	***
Entertainment	→	Utilitarian Motive	−0.438	0.293	−1.492	0.136
Store Atmospherics	→	Hedonic Motive	0.082	0.041	1.978	0.048*
Pricing and Value	→	Hedonic Motive	0.272	0.079	3.424	***
Assortment	→	Hedonic Motive	0.144	0.069	2.079	0.038*
In-Store Delights	→	Hedonic Motive	0.118	0.051	2.313	0.021*
Convenience	→	Hedonic Motive	0.146	0.058	2.503	0.012*
Product/Service Quality and Reliability	→	Hedonic Motive	0.224	0.058	3.86	***
Person-to-Person Experience	→	Hedonic Motive	0.292	0.081	3.608	***
Problem-Solving	→	Hedonic Motive	0.173	0.079	2.195	0.028*
Entertainment	→	Hedonic Motive	−0.191	0.146	−1.311	0.19
Hedonic Motive	→	Patronage Intention	0.859	0.169	5.095	***
Utilitarian Motive	→	Patronage Intention	0.177	0.041	4.283	***

*Significant at 0.05 ($p < 0.05$), **Significant at 0.01 ($p < 0.01$), ***Significant at 0.001 ($p < 0.001$) (CR = t Value)
Source Estimated from Primary Data

Discriminant validity was investigated by comparing the square root of the Average Variance Extracted (AVE) for a specific frame with the relationships between that construct and all other constructs (Hair et al., 1998, 2010). The square roots of the AVEs are more prominent than the off-diagonal elements in the equivalent rows and columns, and they outnumber the relationships between any two constructs in the model. This implies that a construct has a stronger relationship with its indicators than with the other constructs in the model. In Tables 4.6 and 4.9, the diagonal elements in the squared inner construct correlation (SIC) matrix have been replaced by the square roots of the average variance extracted and compared with all AVEs. Further, the AVEs obtained in both scales were compared with the inner construct correlations for each item (Tables 4.6 and 4.9) and found to be greater in all cases. As a result, discriminant validity appears to be satisfactory at the construct level for both scales. Figures 4.1 and 4.2 explain confirmed constructs of consumers' preferred attributes, shopping motivation, and patronage intention in organized retailing (A & B).

Shopping Motivation and Patronage Intention (SMPI) Model
Once the measurement validity of factor structures of consumer preferences, shopping motivation, and patronage intention (SMPI) was assessed, the next thing was testing the global model proposed to explain the pillars of customer-centricity in organized retailing (The PMP Model) concerning consumer shopping behavior and preferences (Fig. 4.3). The reliability and validity of the scales were evaluated during the CFA stage, and the proposed causal model is estimated during this stage, as shown in Fig. 4.4, the path estimates in Table 4.10, and the Goodness-of-Fit indices in Table 4.11.

Structural equation modeling (SEM) was used in this study to investigate the hypothesized linkages in the conceptual framework/proposed model (as shown in Fig. 4.3). Anderson and Gerbing (1988) proposed a two-step method for applying SEM. The first step is to verify the measurement model, followed by the structural model. The measuring model confirms the constructs' unidimensionality, which is analogous to the CFA (Yu & Ramanathan, 2012) described in the previous section. The proposed structural model is next tested by validating structural linkages represented by hypotheses. The following paragraphs provide a detailed description of the structural model depicted in Fig. 4.4.

4 CUSTOMER SEGMENTATION: SMPI MODEL   73

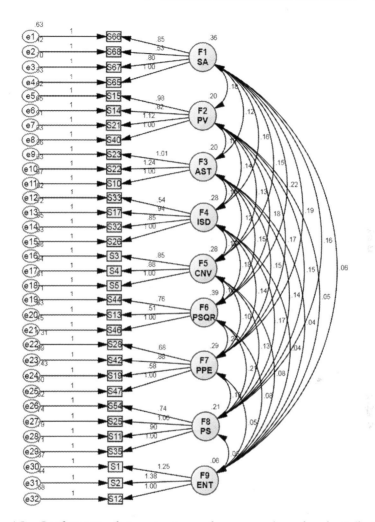

Fig. 4.1 Confirmatory factor structure of consumers' preferred attributes in organized retailing (*NB* SA—Store Atmospherics, P.V.—Pricing and Value, AST—Assortment, ISD—In-store Delights, CNV—Convenience, PSQR—Product/Service Quality and Reliability, PPE—Person-to-Person Experience, P.S.—Problem-Solving, ENT—Entertainment. *Source* Developed by authors in AMOS 20.0 using Primary Data)

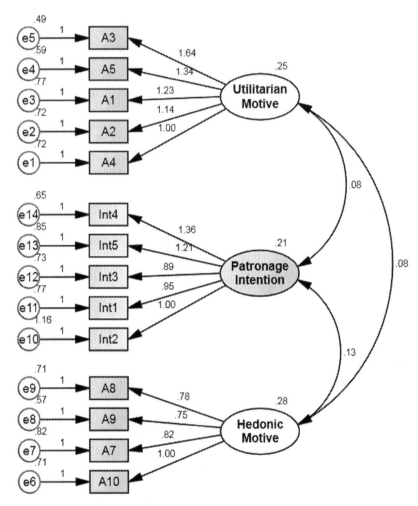

Fig. 4.2 Confirmatory factor structure of consumer shopping motivation and patronage intention in organized retailing (*Source* Developed by authors in AMOS 20.0 using Primary Data. This figure depicts the constructs of consumers' shopping motivation and patronage intention in organized retailing)

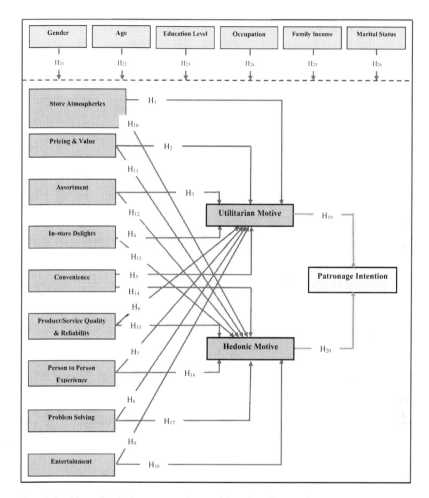

Fig. 4.3 Hypothetical structural model of pillars of customer-centricity: *Preference-Motivation-Patronage (PMP Model)* (*Source* Developed by authors)

The research model is evaluated using Partial Least Squares (PLS). PLS is a structured equation modeling methodology that can analyze SEMs with multiple-item constructs and direct and indirect pathways. PLS derives consecutive linear combinations of predictors efficiently representing both response and predictor variation. PLS is a robust

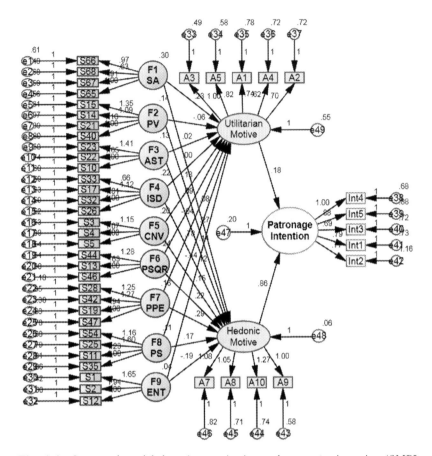

Fig. 4.4 Structural model shopping motivation and patronage intention (SMPI Model) in organized retailing (*Source* Developed by authors in AMOS 20.0 using Primary Data. This figure depicts the structural model of pillars of customer-centricity in organized retailing)

model assessment technique due to its low measurement scales, sample size, and residual distribution requirements. Furthermore, PLS avoids two serious issues: inadmissible solutions and factor indeterminacy. PLS focuses on predicting responses and understanding the underlying relationship between variables. A PLS analysis is divided into two stages:

Table 4.10 Goodness-of-fit of structural model of customer-centricity: PMP model of moderating effects

Demographic attribute	Goodness-of-fit indices
Gender	$\chi^2/\text{df} = 2.550$, $p = 0.000$; NFI = 0.866; GFI = 0.933; CFI = 0.902; RMSEA = 0.048; AGFI = 0.875
Age	$\chi^2/\text{df} = 2.469$, $p = 0.000$); NFI = 0.786; GFI = 0.796; CFI = 0.698; RMSEA = 0.046; AGFI = 0.875
Education	$\chi^2/\text{df} = 2.469$, $p = 0.000$); NFI = 0.786; GFI = 0.796; CFI = 0.698; RMSEA = 0.046; AGFI = 0.845
Occupation	$\chi^2/\text{df} = 2.459$, $p = 0.000$); NFI = 0.886; GFI = 0.896; CFI = 0.798; RMSEA = 0.044; AGFI = 0.849
Family Income	$\chi^2/\text{df} = 2.652$, $p = 0.000$); NFI = 0.862; GFI = 0.856; CFI = 0.769; RMSEA = 0.048; AGFI = 0.817
Martial Status	$\chi^2/\text{df} = 2.572$, $p = 0.000$); NFI = 0.883; GFI = 0.876; CFI = 0.761; RMSEA = 0.042; AGFI = 0.838

(1) the evaluation of the measurement model, which includes the reliability and discriminant validity of the measures, as previously explained in CFA, and (2) the evaluation of the structural model. Figure 4.4 depicts the evaluation of the structural equation model proposed for this study. The proposed model's standardized path coefficients and significance are reported in Table 4.10. These coefficients indicate the effect of one variable on predicting another. The goodness-of-fit indices (also shown in Table 4.11) suggest that the proposed model adequately fits the data. Table 4.11 shows that absolute fit measures, incremental fit measures, and parsimonious fit measures are acceptable. The measurement model's results show acceptable levels of convergent and discriminant validity.

Figure 4.4 and Tables 4.10 and 4.10 show the structural model results obtained with AMOS 20.0. The fit statistics for the model revealed a CMIN/df value of 3.209, CFI of 0.858, GFI of 0.895, and an RMSEA of 0.027, which suggests an acceptable fit of the model to the population (Hu & Bentler, 1999). According to the structural framework of the nine consumer preference dimensions, *store atmospherics* and *problem-solving* reflect consumer shopping motivation in terms of "*utilitarian motive*" and *store atmospherics, pricing and Value, assortment, in-store delights, convenience, product/service quality and reliability, person-to-person experience* and *problem-solving* in terms of "*hedonic motive.*" Further, it

Table 4.11 Summarized result of segmentation of organized retail store shoppers based on moderating effect of consumer demographics on SMPI model of customer-centricity

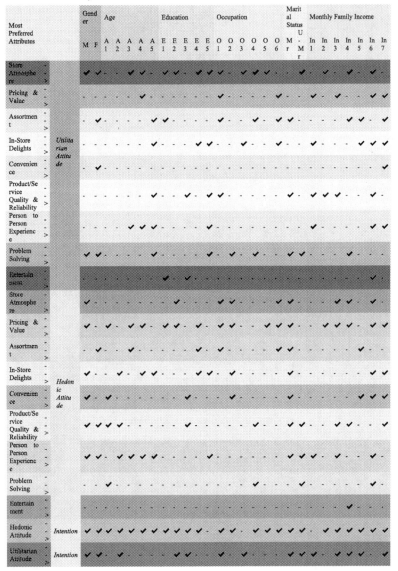

Source Developed by authors (Based on Estimation of Primary Data)

was found that both utilitarian and hedonic shopping motives among shoppers strongly lead to "*patronage intention.*"

Based on the research model, next, the estimate of the path coefficients was performed to test the hypothesis relationships. First, the hypothetical relationships between consumers' preferred attributes/consumer preferences and their shopping motivation were examined. As identified and validated, the two shopping motives were hypothetically linked (H_1 to H_9 and H_{10} to H_{18}) to each consumer preference latent constructs as antecedents of the shopping motivation of customers. When examined, it was found that the utilitarian shopping motive of organized retail shoppers are influenced positively and significantly by consumers' preferred attributes: Shopping Atmospherics (H_1: $\beta = 0.235$, $t = 2.854$, $p < 0.05$) and Problem-Solving (H8: $\beta = 0.776$, $t = 4.114$, $p < 0.0001$). Similarly, the hedonic shopping motive of organized retail shoppers is influenced positively and significantly by consumers' preferred attributes: Store Atmospherics (H10: $\beta = 0.082$, $t = 1.978$, $p < 0.05$), Pricing and Value (H11: $\beta = 0.272$, $t = 3.424$, $p < 0.0001$), Assortment (H12: $\beta = 0.144$, $t = 2.079$, $p < 0.05$), In-store Delights (H13: $\beta = 0.118$, $t = 2.313$, $p < 0.05$), Convenience (H14: $\beta = 0.058$, $t = 2.503$, $p < 0.05$), Product/Service Quality and Reliability (H15: $\beta = 0.224$, $t = 3.86$, $p < 0.0001$), Person-to-Person Experience (H16: $\beta = 0.292$, $t = 3.608$, $p < 0.0001$) and Problem-Solving (H17: $\beta = 0.173$, $t = 2.195$, $p < 0.05$) but surprisingly negatively and not significantly by Entertainment (H5: $\beta = 0.047$, $t = -4.273$, $p < 0.5$). While examining the antecedents of patronage intention and their hypothetical relationship with consumers' shopping motives (utilitarian and hedonic) in an organized retail context, it was found that patronage intention toward super/hypermarket stores (i.e., contained retailing) is influenced positively and significantly by both utilitarian shopping motives of shoppers (H_{19}: $\beta = 0.859$, $t = 5.095$, $p < 0.0001$); and also hedonic shopping motives of consumers (H_{20}: $\beta = 0.177$, $t = 4.283$, $p < 0.0001$). In other words, consumers' utilitarian and hedonic shopping motive strongly and positively leads to patronage intention among super/hypermarket shoppers.

The results summarized in Fig. 4.5 demonstrate significant relationships in hypotheses: H1, H8, H10, H11, H12, H13, H14, H15, H16, H17, H19, and H20. In these cases, the p-value is significant. Hence the null hypothesis is not accepted, and the respective alternative hypotheses are supported.

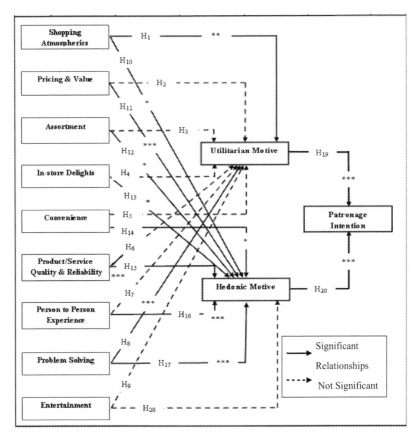

Fig. 4.5 Result of hypotheses testing (*Source* Estimated from Primary Data) (*Significant at 0.05 [$p < 0.05$], **Significant at 0.01 [$p < 0.01$], ***Significant at 0.001 [$p < 0.001$])

The results indicate that both utilitarian and hedonic shopping motivations have significantly favorable effects on patronage intention. Moreover, most notably, consumers' preferred attributes significantly lead to hedonic shopping motives than utilitarian motives. It means what consumers prefer, which leads to their shopping motive and consequently results in customer patronage intention. The result reveals that customers visiting super/hypermarket stores in Odisha are more hedonic rather than utilitarian. This indication hints that utilitarian shoppers preferably visit the small mom-and-pop stores for their need fulfilments. The customers visiting shopping malls/super/hypermarket stores (i.e., organized retail stores) are highly driven by hedonic shopping motives.

Moreover, most importantly, contradicting the notion that entertainment plays a significant role in super/hypermarket shopping or the general conception that entertainment is the antecedent of consumers' mall visits was null from the analysis. It was found that entertainment neither leads to a utilitarian nor hedonic motive in organized retailing. In other words, shoppers do not visit super/hypermarket stores or shopping malls just for the sake of entertainment but rather moreover to accomplish their hedonic shopping motives, which is stemmed from their preferences like—Store Atmospherics, Pricing and Value, Assortment, In-Store Delights, Convenience, Product/Service Quality & Reliability, Person-to-Person Experience and Problem-Solving.

Moderating Effects of Consumer Demographics on the SMPI Model

Many moderating effects on the relationship between consumer preferences, shopping motivation, and patronage intention have been identified and tested in super/hypermarket store (i.e., offline) environments. However, the geographical region in which this study is being carried out in India has not received any identifiable research attention about organized retailing. The concept of customer-centricity has not received that much attention in India even. Consumer demographics and engagement are expected to hold in the offline environment about critical consumer decision-making. Examining the causal model on the complete sample of organized retail buyers allows for contrasting the significance of the direct correlations explored in Hypotheses 1–20. As a result, using the AMOS 20.0 statistical software, a set of multi-sample models was estimated to examine the moderating effects of consumers' demographic characteristics on their preferences, shopping motivation, and patronage intention (Hypotheses 21–26). This methodology helps evaluate the adequacy of a factor structure between different groups by statistically examining the equality of the aspects measured by the structural model between the proposed groups (Bentler & Bonett, 1980; Kline, 2011). For these statistics, the causal model should include several constraints that equal the structural characteristics of all groups being examined, as illustrated in Fig. 4.6. Tables 4.7 contain the results, and Table 4.9 summarizes the significant results. To assess the moderating impacts of consumers' demographic features, a multi-sample analysis was undertaken for each category: gender, age, education, occupation, marital status, and family income. The AMOS-generated model is depicted in Fig. 4.6.

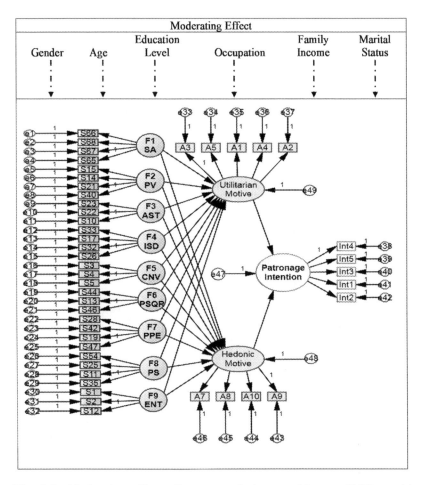

Fig. 4.6 Moderating effect of consumers' demographics on SMPI model (*Source* Developed by authors in AMOS 20.0 with Insights from Primary Data Analysis)

According to *gender*, consumers have been classified into two categories, male (M) and female (F), for *Age* four types: below 20—A1, 21 to 30—A2, 31 to 40—A3, 41, and above as A4 (41 to 50 and Above 51 category was merged and regrouped as 41 and above); for *Education* four groups: above P.G.—E1, P.G.—E2, Graduate—E3, Intermediate or below—E4 (the matriculation or below category was merged in intermediate or below category); similarly for *Occupation* five sub-sample groups: govt. Employee—O1, business—O2, students—O3 (the unemployed subgroup was merged with students), private sector employees—O4 and housewife—O5; for *Marital Status*, two sub-sample groups: married—Mr, unmarried—U Mr; and finally considering their *Family Income* five sub-sample groups: below 15,000—In1, 15,001 to 30,000—In2, 30,001 to 45,000—In3, 45,001 to 60,000—In4 and 60,001 or above as In5 (as depicted in Table 4.11). The results obtained through multi-sample models that analyze the moderating effects of consumers' demographic characteristics are depicted in Table 4.11. In all of the analyses performed, the goodness of fit indices obtained from the multi-sample models indicated below each Table show values close to the suggested thresholds. Furthermore, the structural coefficients and the Lagrange multiplier test results (p values) show a significant variation in the impact of consumers' demography factors on consumer preferences, shopping motivation, and patronage intention in the context of organized retailing.

The summarized findings of a multi-sample analysis to explore the moderating effect of the main demographic factors of consumers on the PMP model of customer-centricity are shown in Table 4.10 (which can otherwise be termed segmentation of organized retail store shoppers based on demographics). The results show that users' gender, occupation, and monthly income significantly determine organized retail preferences and shopping motivation. However, the users' age, education, and marital status influence the factors determining online purchasing intention. Regarding shoppers' gender, the preference factors like Shopping Atmospherics and Problem-Solving lead to utilitarian shopping motives. Product/Service Quality and Reliability and Person-to-Person Experience lead to hedonic shopping motives for both males and females. As per the result, utilitarian and hedonic shopping motivation significantly leads to patronage intention for super/hypermarket shoppers.

Pricing and Value, and Person Experience are more critical for shoppers' hedonic shopping motivation regarding shoppers' age. Regarding the users' education level, Store Atmospherics is essential for utilitarian shopping motives, and Pricing and Value is vital for hedonic shopping motives. In shoppers' occupations, Store Atmospherics and Assortment are important for utilitarian shopping motives, and Pricing and Value is significantly essential for hedonic shopping motives. Regarding shoppers' marital status, the preference factor Problem-Solving is crucial for utilitarian shopping motive and Product/Service Quality and Reliability and Person-to-Person Experience, leading to hedonic shopping motives in married and unmarried categories. Regarding monthly family income, Product/Service Quality and Reliability is significantly important across income groups for leading to a utilitarian shopping motive. Pricing & Value are most important for leading to hedonic shopping motives among shoppers across income groups.

The Implication of Research Work

The findings of this study strengthen the existing literature and add new knowledge to it. This research work also contributes to the academic study, research method, and practice which are the novelty of this study. From a theoretical perspective, the main contributions are discussed below:

Over the past few years, several studies have been conducted to identify consumer preference attributes in the context of large-format organized retailing. This study has narrowed the gap of previous research investigating consumer preference attributes in a large format of organized retailing and identified nine consumer preference factors in organized retail stores. To the best of my knowledge, this is the first study conducted in an Indian context related to large-format organized retailing/mall shopping. Principal Component Factor Analysis (PCFA) and Confirmatory Factor Analysis (CFA) develop and validate the factors. In the last decades, several conceptual models have been developed to explain the behavior of organized retail consumers. However, no such discussion in literature is available related to organized retail consumers' preferred attributes and their direct or indirect relationship with consumers' shopping motivation, patronage intention, and customer-centricity. This study proposed an evaluation model for evaluating the interrelationship among the major prime factors in the organized retail context with shopping motivation and patronage intention. This study develops a hypothetical structural model (PMP Model of customer-centricity) of organized retail store consumers' preferred attributes, shopping motivation, and patronage intention to establish an interrelationship and finds the moderating effect of demographic characteristics of consumers employing the Structural Equation Modeling (SEM) approach.

From a practical standpoint, the findings highlight organized retail consumer preference factors that may assist large-format brick-and-mortar retailers in better understanding super/hypermarket shoppers, building strong relationships with them, adequately knowing their needs, and increasing successful transactions and yield patronage. This study is endowed with vast managerial implications for organized retail store managers.

- The identified and validated consumer preference constructs can be used as a baseline for providing a seamless consumer experience.
- The SMPI model of customer-centricity can be used for strategy formulation. It provides deep knowledge on which preference factor motivates consumers in a utilitarian or hedonic way and leads to patronage. The sophisticated segmentation emerged from path analysis of the moderating effect of demographic characteristics to target the right customers.
- The relative prioritization of consumers' and retailers' preferences provides ample knowledge about mismatches between customers' priorities and retailers' strategies and offerings.

Conclusion

Diversity in India is both an opportunity and a formidable challenge for marketers worldwide. If understood correctly, India's demography and diverse culture can be a boon for marketers. However, regardless of product line or service, a little ignorance or faulty assessment can lead to a disastrous situation for business houses, and retailing is not an exception. A trace of Indian diversity can be found in every Indian state, varying significantly from one to the next. As a result, marketers must thoroughly understand each Indian state's consumer culture. The current research work opens the door for future researchers to delve deeper into the subject. Cross-national/cultural studies may be conducted to validate the Preference-Motivation-Patronage (PMP) Model for customer-centricity. Because customer-centricity is becoming increasingly important, research may be performed by considering other business sectors/industries.

A customer-centric strategy is essential in today's retail environment. Marketers must understand their target consumers' decision-making styles across contexts, enhance strategic marketing initiatives, and develop effective communication to support consumer preferences. Changes in previously developed dimensions may be required because of a paradigm shift in retail consumer preferences, behavior, and decision-making style. This research provides a completer and more accurate picture of consumer preferences, shopping motivations, and patronage intention. With the help of a Structural Equation Modeling (SEM) approach, this study investigated the measurement instruments of consumer preferences and attempted to provide optimum solutions to organized retailers to target and segment their consumers in an organized retail platform. The findings of this study benefit marketers, consumers, and academics.

The recent economic downturn and uneven recovery have heightened the need to respond to change more quickly and dramatically. In such volatile market conditions, organized retailers must understand subtle shifts in competitor movements and new consumer behavior and preferences to adopt a business model. They must acclimate to the proposed path to customer-centric retailing and make critical improvements to their mode of operation through continuous monitoring. Ultimately, customer-centric businesses will thrive because they strive for a balance of equity and efficiency, ensuring that buyers and sellers benefit from their transactions and relationships. Retail entities that can gain a competitive advantage by adopting a Customer-Centric Business Model (CCBM) will be competitive today and will continue to win tomorrow.

Acknowledgements Manoj Kumar Dash and Manash Kumar Sahu collected data for the study. The data collection was not funded.

References

Anderson, J. C., & Gerbing, D. W. (1988). Structural equation modeling in practice: A review and recommended two-step approach. *Psychological Bulletin*, *103*(3), 411–423. https://doi.org/10.1037/0033-2909.103.3.411

Arnold, M. J., & Reynolds, K. E. (2003). Hedonic shopping motivations. *Journal of Retailing*, *79*(2), 77–95. https://doi.org/10.1016/S0022-4359(03)00007-1

Babin, B. J., Darden, W. R., & Griffin, M. (1994). Work and/or fun: Measuring hedonic and utilitarian shopping value. *Journal of Consumer Research*, 20(4), 644–656. https://doi.org/10.1086/209376

Bagozzi, R. P., & Yi, Y. (1988). On the evaluation of structural equation models. *Journal of the Academy of Marketing Science*, 16(1), 74–94. https://doi.org/10.1007/BF02723327

Bentler, P. M., & Bonett, D. G. (1980). Significance tests and goodness of fit in the analysis of covariance structures. *Psychological Bulletin*, 88(3), 588–606. https://doi.org/10.1037/0033-2909.88.3.588

Bhatnagar, A., Misra, S., & Rao, H. R. (2000). On risk, convenience, and Internet shopping behavior. *Communications of the ACM*, 43(11), 98–105. https://doi.org/10.1145/353360.353371

Bhattacharyya, J., Balaji, M. S., & Jiang, Y. (2023). Causal complexity of sustainable consumption: Unveiling the equifinal causes of purchase intentions of plant-based meat alternatives. *Journal of Business Research*, 156, 113511. https://doi.org/10.1016/j.jbusres.2022.113511

Byrne, B. M. (2001). Structural equation modeling with AMOS, EQS, and LISREL: Comparative approaches to testing for the factorial validity of a measuring instrument. *International Journal of Testing*, 1(1), 55–86. https://doi.org/10.1207/S15327574IJT0101_4

Comrey, A. L., & Lee, H. B. (1992). *A first course in factor analysis* (2nd ed). Lawrence Erlbaum Associates.

Dabholkar, P. A. (1995). *A contingency framework for predicting causality between customer satisfaction and service quality*. ACR North American advances.

Dawson, S., Bloch, P. H., & Ridgway, N. (1990). Shopping motives, emotional states, and. *Journal of Retailing*, 66(4), 408–427.

Field, A. (2000). *Discovering statistics using SPSS for Windows*. SAGE.

Fornell, C., & Bookstein, F. L. (1982). Two structural equation models: LISREL and PLS applied to consumer exit-voice theory. *Journal of Marketing Research*, 19(4), 440–452. https://doi.org/10.1177/002224378201900406

Fornell, C., & Larcker, D. F. (1981). Structural equation models with unobservable variables and measurement error: Algebra and statistics. *Journal of Marketing Research*, 18(3), 382–388. https://doi.org/10.1177/002224378101800313

Gebauer, H., & Kowalkowski, C. (2012). Customer-focused and service-focused orientation in organizational structures. *Journal of Business and Industrial Marketing*, 27(7), 527–537. https://doi.org/10.1108/08858621211257293

Hair, J. F., Black, W. C., Babin, B. J., Anderson, R. E., & Tatham, R. L. (1998). *Multivariate data analysis* (5th ed., No. 3, pp. 207–219). Upper Saddle River.

Hair, J. F., Black, W. C., Babin, B. J., Anderson, R. E., & Tatham, R. L. (2010). *Multivariate data analysis* (Vol. 7). Prentice Hall.

Hienerth, C., Keinz, P., & Lettl, C. (2011). Exploring the nature and implementation process of user-centric business models. *Long Range Planning*, *44*(5–6), 344–374. https://doi.org/10.1016/j.lrp.2011.09.009

Homburg, C., Workman, J. P., & Jensen, O. (2000). Fundamental changes in marketing organization: The movement toward a customer-focused organizational structure. *Journal of the Academy of Marketing Science*, *28*(4), 459–478. https://doi.org/10.1177/0092070300284001

Hu, L. T., & Bentler, P. M. (1999). Cutoff criteria for fit indexes in covariance structure analysis: Conventional criteria versus new alternatives. *Structural Equation Modeling: A Multidisciplinary Journal*, *6*(1), 1–55. https://doi.org/10.1080/10705519909540118

Jin, B., & Kim, J. O. (2003). A typology of Korean discount shoppers: Shopping motives, store attributes, and outcomes. *International Journal of Service Industry Management*, *14*(4), 396–419. https://doi.org/10.1108/09564230310489240

Khare, A. (2012). Impact of consumer decision–making styles on Indian consumers' mall shopping behaviour. *International Journal of Indian Culture and Business Management*, *5*(3), 259–279. https://doi.org/10.1504/IJICBM.2012.046624

Kline, R. (2011). *Convergence of structural equation modeling and multilevel modeling*. Sage. https://doi.org/10.4135/9781446268261

Korgaonkar, P. K., & Wolin, L. D. (1999). A multivariate analysis of web usage. *Journal of Advertising Research*, *39*(2), 53–53.

Kuruvilla, S. J., & Joshi, N. (2010). Influence of demographics, psychographics, shopping orientation, mall shopping attitude and purchase patterns on mall patronage in India. *Journal of Retailing and Consumer Services*, *17*(4), 259–269. https://doi.org/10.1016/j.jretconser.2010.02.003

Lamberti, L. (2013). Customer centricity: The construct and the operational antecedents. *Journal of Strategic Marketing*, *21*(7), 588–612. https://doi.org/10.1080/0965254X.2013.817476

Lee, J. Y., Sridhar, S., Henderson, C. M., & Palmatier, R. W. (2015). Effect of customer-centric structure on long-term financial performance. *Marketing Science*, *34*(2), 250–268. https://doi.org/10.1287/mksc.2014.0878

Leszczyc, P. T. L. P., Sinha, A., & Timmermans, H. J. P. (2000). Consumer store choice dynamics: An analysis of the competitive market structure for grocery stores. *Journal of Retailing*, *76*(3), 323–345. https://doi.org/10.1016/S0022-4359(00)00033-6

Lysonski, S., & Durvasula, S. (2013). Consumer decision making styles in retailing: Evolution of mindsets and psychological impacts. *Journal of*

Consumer Marketing, *30*(1), 75–87. https://doi.org/10.1108/073637613 11290858

Malhotra, N. K., & Dash, S. (2011). *Marketing research an applied orientation.* Pearson Publishing.

Michel, J. W., Tews, M. J., & Kavanagh, M. J. (2014). Development and validation of the Customer-Centered Behavior measure. *Service Industries Journal*, *34*(13), 1075–1091. https://doi.org/10.1080/02642069.2014.939640

Mittal, V., & Kamakura, W. A. (2001). Satisfaction, repurchase intent, and repurchase behavior: Investigating the moderating effect of customer characteristics. *Journal of Marketing Research*, *38*(1), 131–142. https://doi.org/10.1509/jmkr.38.1.131.18832

Nunnally, J. C. (1978). An overview of psychological measurement. In B. B. Wolman (Ed.), *Clinical diagnosis of mental disorders* (97–146). Springer. https://doi.org/10.1007/978-1-4684-2490-4_4

Parasuraman, A., Zeithaml, V. A., & Berry, L. L. (1988). SERVQUAL: A multiple-item scale for measuring consumer perceptions of service quality. *Journal of Marketing*, *64*, 12–40.

Peppers, D., & Rogers, M. (2012). Strategic marketing. In J. Kourdi (Ed.), *The marketing century: How marketing drives business and shapes society* (pp. 19–25). Wiley.

Rajagopal. (2011). Determinants of shopping behavior of urban consumers. *Journal of International Consumer Marketing*, *23*(2), 83–104. https://doi.org/10.1080/08961530.2011.543051

Ranaweera, C., McDougall, G., & Bansal, H. (2005). A model of online customer behavior during the initial transaction: Moderating effects of customer characteristics. *Marketing Theory*, *5*(1), 51–74. https://doi.org/10.1177/1470593105049601

Shah, D., Rust, R. T., Parasuraman, A., Staelin, R., & Day, G. S. (2006). The path to customer centricity. *Journal of Service Research*, *9*(2), 113–124. https://doi.org/10.1177/1094670506294666

Shenoy, S. S., Sequeira, A. H., & Devaraj, K. (2012). Service quality: The cornerstone of customer-centric retail strategy for supermarket retailers in India [Electronic resource]. *International Journal of Marketing and Business Communication*, 11–17.

Sheth, J. N., Sethia, N. K., & Srinivas, S. (2011). Mindful consumption: A customer-centric approach to sustainability. *Journal of the Academy of Marketing Science*, *39*(1), 21–39. https://doi.org/10.1007/s11747-010-0216-3

Sheth, J. N., Sisodia, R. S., & Sharma, A. (2000). The antecedents and consequences of customer-centric marketing. *Journal of the Academy of Marketing Science*, *28*(1), 55–66. https://doi.org/10.1177/0092070300281006

Singh, D. P. (2015). Effect of shopping motivations on Indian consumers' mall patronage intention. *Asia-Pacific Journal of Management Research and Innovation*, *11*(1), 57–65. https://doi.org/10.1177/2319510X14565040

Sirgy, M. J., Grewal, D., & Mangleburg, T. (2000). Retail environment, self-congruity, and retail patronage. *Journal of Business Research*, *49*(2), 127–138. https://doi.org/10.1016/S0148-2963(99)00009-0

Tauber, E. M. (1972). Marketing notes and communications: Why do people shop? *Journal of Marketing*, *36*(4), 46–49. https://doi.org/10.1177/002224297203600409

Taylor, S., & Todd, P. (1995). Decomposition and crossover effects in the theory of planned behavior: A study of consumer adoption intentions. *International Journal of Research in Marketing*, *12*(2), 137–155. https://doi.org/10.1016/0167-8116(94)00019-K38

Voss, K. E., Spangenberg, E. R., & Grohmann, B. (2003). Measuring the hedonic and utilitarian dimensions of consumer attitude. *Journal of Marketing Research*, *40*(3), 310–320. https://doi.org/10.1509/jmkr.40.3.310.19238

Westbrook, R. A., & Black, W. C. (1985). A motivation-based shopper typology. *Journal of Retailing*, *61*(1), 78–103.

Wu, L. Y., Wang, C. J., Tseng, C. Y., & Wu, M. C. (2009). Founding team and start-up competitive advantage. *Management Decision*, *47*(2), 345–358. https://doi.org/10.1108/00251740910938957

Xia, L., & Sudharshan, D. (2002). Effects of interruptions on consumer online decision processes. *Journal of Consumer Psychology*, *12*(3), 265–280. https://doi.org/10.1207/S15327663JCP1203_08

Yu, W., & Ramanathan, R. (2012). Retail service quality, corporate image and behavioural intentions: The mediating effects of customer satisfaction. *International Review of Retail, Distribution and Consumer Research*, *22*(5), 485–505. https://doi.org/10.1080/09593969.2012.711250

Zhang, J., & Breugelmans, E. (2012). The impact of an item-based loyalty program on consumer purchase behavior. *Journal of Marketing Research*, *49*(1), 50–65. https://doi.org/10.1509/jmr.09.0211

CHAPTER 5

Strategic Mismatch: IAHP

INTRODUCTION

Modern retail is experiencing unprecedented disruption and change due to various new retail channels and mobile and digital technologies. A convenience store in Seattle, Washington, self-service Amazon Go is one of the most recent examples substantiating this claim. The Amazon Go case exemplifies the potential threat the convenience stores, grocery stores, and fast food outlets may face shortly. Amazon Go's future expansion has the potential to disrupt the broader retail industry and has a significant impact on millions of retail employees (Ives et al., 2019). With these rapid changes in mind, it is time for retailers to become highly responsive to customers and customer-centric while positioning themselves for future retailing. This necessitates ensuring that retailers provide the appropriate resources and services following their customers' expectations.

In today's market disruption, retailers who can nimble, adapt, and innovate their business model and implement a customer-centric business model (CCBM) will be better prepared to succeed. The roadmap provided in this study, backed by empirical evidence, can be used directly by large-format organized retail stores to instill customer-centricity. When practiced and managed correctly, customer-centricity confers individuality—distinguishing oneself from competitors. Customer-centricities

© The Author(s), under exclusive license to Springer Nature
Singapore Pte Ltd. 2023
M. K. Dash et al., *Customer-Centricity in Organized Retailing*,
https://doi.org/10.1007/978-981-19-3593-0_5

have been discussed as a concept for more than a half-century. The existing literature heavily emphasizes the importance of aligning with the customer-centric paradigm (Shah et al., 2006). Customer-centricity has emerged as an emerging research area in the last decade, with massive company reports on this specific concept being published and literature on retailing demonstrating a gradual increase (Anderson et al., 2007). With the swift advancement of technology and the high market dynamics of India, more businesses are making efforts to become customer-centric to entice, align, and retain their customers. Customer-centricity is an easy way to boost "Customer Lifetime Value (CLV)" by discovering new and innovative ways to serve valuable customers (Fader, 2012). Despite its growing significance, current knowledge of customer-centricity is limited; specifically, there is evidence of very little research on customer-centricity (There is no such study that is backed up by empirical evidence.) in the context of organized retailing, as well as limitations in current knowledge of how the roadmap for adopting and implementing customer-centricity unfolds.

The study's premise is based on the marketers' prerequisite to understand their consumers' decision-making styles across the contexts, develop effective communication to support consumer preferences, and progress the strategic marketing activities. The paradigm shift in retail consumer preferences, behavior, and decision-making may necessitate adjustments to previously developed dimensions. To accomplish this, our study investigated consumer preference measurement instruments and attempted to provide optimum solutions to organized retailers to target by prioritizing consumer preferences and retailers' strategic responses using the Analytical Hierarchy Process (AHP) approach.

The overarching goal of the present study is to prioritize customer-preferred factors in organized retailing. On the other hand, prioritizing consumers' preferences will not be fruitful for retailers unless retailers' counter-strategies to appease their customer base are prioritized. The primary goal of prioritizing retailers' relevant counter-strategies regarding customers' preferences is to observe any mismatches between the string of consumers' preferences and retailers' responses. This study looks at the priority hierarchy of preferences from the customer's point of view and the relevant strategies for addressing those preferences from the retailer's point of view. The study focuses on how retailers respond to constantly changing consumer preferences, which strategies are being implemented by large-format organized retailers on which priority basis, and whether this corresponds to the consumers' priorities. Prioritizing the strategy for organized retailers requires determining the roles and preferences of customers. With shifting consumer tastes and preferences in today's business environment, retail strategy is a complex process involving many criteria. Strategy formulation and decision-making become difficult in such a complex situation. To respond to such a complex situation, a statistical tool known as Analytical Hierarchy Process (AHP) is used in the present study.

Furthermore, an effort has been made to understand the priorities of consumers and retail strategy makers. This study will contribute to a more inclusive understanding of customer-centricity and lay the groundwork for future empirical research on customer-centricity in an organized retail setting. As a result, we are adding to the existing literature on organized retailing.

As a result, the focus of the work is to examine the two distinct issues separately.

i. To prioritization of consumer preferences dimension (Consumer perspective)
ii. To prioritization of retailers' counter-strategies (Retailers' Perspective)
iii. To compare the prioritizes of Consumer Preference and Retailers' Perspective and to suggest a model for increase crowd in the retail marketplace

The rest of the chapter is structured as follows. The relevant literature is discussed in the first section to provide context for our empirical study. The second section describes in detail the research method and methodology followed in the study. The third section comprises discussions of the research findings. Finally, the fourth section concludes the study by stating the study's limitations and opening up future research avenues.

Consumer Decision-Making Models

According to Sproles (1985), consumer decision-making styles are patterned, mental, cognitive ordinations that constantly supervise a consumer's approach to making choices about shopping and purchasing, resulting in the development of a lasting personality by the consumer (Sprotles & Kendall, 1986).

Out of many available models, the three proposed, well-established "comprehensive" models by Howard and Sheth (1969), Engel et al. (1968), and Nicosia (1966) are prominent. These researchers, through their models, attempt to trace individual consumers' psychological states through which they attempt to satisfy and address their needs by buying what they require. Engel et al. (1986) claim that an extensive problem-solving process with high product involvement could be needed. The process comprises a step-by-step process that initiates information search, alternative evaluation, purchase, and post-purchase activities. In-depth processing of all possible information supports the process. The results of such in-depth information processing are expected to be highly satisfying. Festinger (1957) was the first to present cognitive dissonance theory to consumers, influencing future purchasing. According to Engel and Blackwell (1982), the environment can influence the decision process by influencing the consumer's motivation and intent. Unpredictable factors may influence the final decision. Consumer decision-making has become much more complicated over time as a result of a greater variety of products available (choice overload), information overload and ambiguity, and technological advancements (Chernev et al., 2015; Walsh et al., 2007; Wang & Shukla, 2013), greater bargaining power of working women who influence family purchasing decisions (Belch & Willis, 2002), and global influences (Akaka & Alden, 2010; Guo, 2013; Newman et al., 2012). As a result, generalizations of consumer decision-making based on traditional decision models are no longer feasible and are thought to be less accurate.

The Criticisms of Consumer Decision-Making Styles

A few researchers disapprove of the CDMS for various reasons ranging from the model fit to the generalization issues of the idea. Consumers' assumption of being complex and rational decision-makers is among the most common criticisms leveled at extended problem-solving models (Olshavsky & Granbois, 1979). However, Ehrenberg (1988) disapproved of these models because the testing could not be done precisely on these models, and there is no specific establishment of relationships between the concepts. Also, there are no accepted methods to measure them. Olshavsky and Granbois (1979) suggest that generalizing this model to most consumers' purchase decisions is impossible. Further to add, the solutions and models of decision-making discussed in the later parts of the chapter are made to understand the behavior in purchase situations of consumers who are not highly involved and do not engage in the rigorous problem-solving approach.

THE PRESCRIBED SOLUTIONS

According to Engel et al. (1968), the distinguishment of cognitive activity caused by purchasing by using the concept of "high" and "low" involvement was first done by Krugman (1965). According to many consumer research, consumers' capacity to receive and use information is limited (e.g., Jacoby et al., 1977). They do not, on average, conduct rational, comparative assessments of brands based on their attributes or make final decisions among the brands based on complex information processing outputs such as intentions and attitudes. Usually, customers are not keen on searching for information or spending their time rigorously evaluating each alternative when engaging in a limited problem-solving process; instead, they make simple decision rules to choose between alternatives (Pachauri, 2001).

According to Pachauri (2001), the level of consumer involvement and differentiation of the product or service can explain the level of effort expended in any decision-making.

The consumer typology approach classifies consumers into types based on motives and attitudes of consumers' shopping (Darden & Ashton, 1974; Moschis, 1976). While according to Sprotles and Kendall (1986) and Sproles and Sproles (1990), the cognitive and affective orientations related to consumer decision-making are defined by the consumer characteristics approach. Psychographic research postulates that consumer personalities and predicts consumer behavior can be effectively measured by consumers' activity, interest, and opinion statements (Lastovicka, 1982; Wells, 2011). The consumer characteristics approach has been deemed the most powerful and explanatory of the three approaches because its main focus is on the mental orientation of the consumer in the decision-making process. Sprotles and Kendall (1986) have bought up a collective approach of these and other traits to create the Consumer Styles Inventory (CSI), which is essentially a list of consumer decision-making styles. Sprotles and Kendall (1986) developed the consumer-style inventory based on a hypothetical thought that eight central decision-making styles can explain consumer decision-making behavior that is: high-quality conscious consumer, brand consciousness, novelty and fashion-conscious, recreational and shopping conscious, price-conscious, impulsiveness, confused by over-choice, brand loyal (Sprotles & Kendall, 1986).

Following the results of Sprotles and Kendall (1986), Hari et al. (2009) attempted to understand the decision-making styles of Indian consumers in shopping malls through their research; the results suggested that six decision-making styles are relevant in the Indian context, they are

1. Price consciousness,
2. Quality consciousness,
3. Recreational,
4. Confused by over-choice,
5. Novelty consciousness, and
6. Variety seeking.

Their research rejected the applicability of the four dimensions proposed, i.e.,

1. Fashion consciousness,
2. Brand consciousness,
3. Impulsiveness, and
4. Brand loyalty.

The consumer decision-making styles of Indian consumers' mall shopping behavior were studied by Khare (2012). According to Khare (2012), the age of the consumers influences their purchasing habits, and the mall shopping attributes were found to be affected by novelty-seeking, brand-conscious, and recreational shopping styles.

Hoffman and Turley (2002) conducted a study on "Atmospherics, Service Encounters, and Consumer Decision Making: An Integrative Perspective" with two purposes. Then, they addressed the atmospherics' roles in the consumer decision processes within service encounters. In their study, Wesley et al. (2006) used a comparative method to examine the relationship between consumers' decision-making styles, shopping mall behavior, and overall evaluations of shopping malls. Lysonski and Durvasula (2013) used a framework of consumer decision-making styles.

The 2009 data was also analyzed cross-sectionally to see if decision-making styles are influenced by psychological variables such as shopping opinion leadership, perceived time pressure, shopping self-confidence, consumer susceptibility to interpersonal influence, and materialism influence. It is investigated by Wanninayake (2014) if there is any impact of consumer decision-making styles on their preference for domestic brands in the Czech public and the results of fashion consciousness, impulsiveness, recreational orientation, and price consciousness of consumers display a direct relationship with domestic brand biasness.

Complex Decision-Making and MCDM

Making decisions is one of the most challenging tasks we face daily. The major problem is that, generally, all the decision problems have multiple, often conflicting criteria (Bhattacharyya et al., 2023). Such issues are broadly classified as Multiple Attribute Decision-Making (MADM) and Multiple Objective Decision-Making (MODM) (Hwang & Yoon, 1981). MADM is associated with problems with a predetermined number of alternatives (Chen & Hwang, 1992; Hwang & Yoon, 1981). The Decision-Maker (DM) chooses/prioritizes/ranks a limited number of options. At the same time, MODM is not related to problems where the alternatives are fixed (Chen & Hwang, 1992; Hwang & Yoon, 1981). The decision-maker's primary concern is to design a "most" promising alternative concerning limited resources (Hwang & Yoon, 1981). The study extends in the context of MADM. Researchers have highlighted the use of Multi-Criteria Decision-Making (MCDM) models (Motakiaee, 2011; Mühlbacher & Kaczynski, 2016; Zamarrón-Mieza et al., 2017). MCDM seeks to improve decision quality by having a clearer process, balanced and effective. It is all about the structuring and solving of multi-criteria decision-making problems.

Consumer Shopping Behavior and Preferences

The Research Gaps

Decision-making has become increasingly complex in today's fast-paced business environment. In today's business, there are inherent and highly complex decision-making problems involving many variables. In today's business world, a decision must be based on several criteria rather than a single criterion. This necessitates assessing various criteria and evaluating alternatives based on each criterion, followed by combining these evaluations to regulate the relative ranking of the alternatives concerning the problem. To reduce the compounded effect of business problems, retailers must address customers' prioritized preferences and identify and prioritize counter-strategies to address their preferences. As a result, the study's rationale is being built.

Furthermore, the existing literature review discovered a notable scarcity regarding Multi-Criteria Decision-Making (MCDM) applicability for handling customer-centricity in organized retail stores. Increased market competition and customers' changing needs and desires for customized products and services point to the need for a customer-focused marketing strategy to meet customer needs. However, there is ambiguity and a lack of understanding in the literature about consumer preferences, decision-making style, loyalty, and retailers' strategy priorities to address the same. Researchers paid no particular attention to learning about consumers' preferences for organized retail store purchases and retailers' counterstrategies. This study fills a gap by developing two priority hierarchy models to understand the importance of consumers' and retailers' preferences related to purchases in organized retail stores and providing knowledge and variability of the interrelationship between factors and sub-factors/strategies. As previously stated, the upcoming section discusses the research methodology employed.

To summarize the study method, the outline of the whole methodological process adopted in this study is presented in Table 5.1.

Firstly, the identified and validated factor structure was considered for prioritizing the customers' preferred factors and sub-factors. Secondly, for prioritizing the counter-strategies, probable and most fitted strategies for each factor and sub-strategies for each variable in the construct were first identified through "expert mining." The methodology as prescribed for AHP was used for further analysis. The second phase of the analysis bears crucial importance as it is the real managerial solution for customer preferences, promoting customer-centricity. In this phase, the consumers' preferred factors and sub-factors were deeply interpreted by experts (retail store managers and floor executives, faculty members and research scholars), called "expert mining," and the relevant set of strategies sub-strategies was then prioritized. The set of counter-strategies was gleaned from expert mining through thorough interpretation and then prioritized, and it is logically named "Interpretive AHP (iAHP)."

Table 5.1 Research process

Objective 1	*Prioritization of consumer preferences & retailers' strategies*	Methodology	Mathematical formulation of AHP Estimation Procedure Factor/sub-factor identification/specifications & decomposition of problem Survey procedure, data & software	
		Step 1 Consumer perspective	Prioritization of consumers' preferred factors: local & global weight Consistency ratio (CR)	AHP
		Step 2 Retailers' perspective	Prioritization of retailers' counter-strategies: local & global weight Consistency ratio (CR)	*i*AHP

Firstly, to *prioritize the customers' preferred factors* and sub-factors, the identified and validated factor

Research Methodology

The Choice of AHP

The methodology is intended to prioritize consumer-preferred factors and sub-factors and retailers' counter-strategies and sub-strategies to make a comparative assessment on a priority basis from a consumer and retailer perspective, for which a mathematical prioritization method Analytic Hierarchy Process (AHP) is used. Retailers use AHP, but it is logically referred to as Interpretive AHP (iAHP) because retailers' strategies and sub-strategies are explored through expert mining's interpretation of consumer preference factors and sub-factors. Figure 5.1 shows the research process followed in the study.

Alternatives to the AHP

Before deciding on a research paradigm, the authors considered various alternative research methods during the formative stage of the research. TOPSIS, DEMATEL, and the use of questionnaire surveys were among those mentioned. However, none of these have the capability of prioritizing. Because of its stepwise comparison mechanism, capability to reduce inconsistency (Jackson, 2001), and appropriateness in our research design, AHP could perform. The following sections provide a technical overview of AHP to help you reflect on the method selection rationale.

AHP: A Technical Overview

Decision-making problems are notoriously difficult to solve because they typically involve multiple criteria (Chen et al., 1992). The difficulty grows in proportion to the qualitative nature of the criteria (Chen et al., 1992). In the context of MCDM problem-solving, quantifying such qualitative variables has always resulted in inconclusive results and a lack of consensus among existing literature. In the 1970s and 1980s, Saaty (1978, 1980a) pioneered the Analytic Hierarchy Process for dealing with such MCDM problems (AHP). Following the development of AHP (Saaty, 1978, 1980a), it was used to solve MCDM problems and is still widely used in the literature.

According to Eroglu (2013), and Saaty (1980a), for representing the elements of any problem hierarchically, the Analytic Hierarchy Process (AHP) is a systematic procedure. AHP is a simple method (Saaty, 1980a,

5 STRATEGIC MISMATCH: IAHP 101

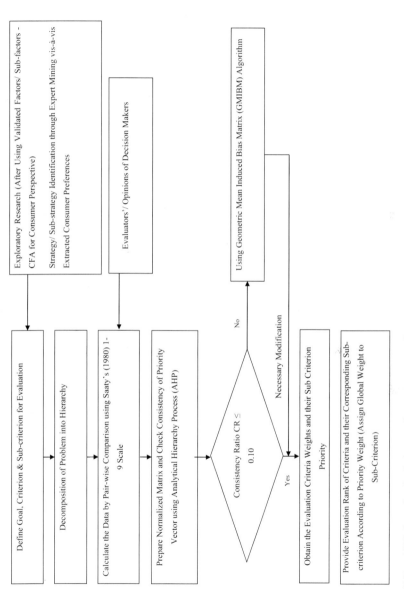

Fig. 5.1 AHP-based calculation and prioritization flow diagram

2000). As a result, the technique is straightforward to use and implement in a decision-making scenario. AHP provides a framework for decision-making processes with limited options, but each has several characteristics. AHP can analyze the MCDM problem by establishing a hierarchy of quantitative or qualitative criteria and sub-criteria. It is possible to accomplish this by introducing a pair-wise comparison between the criteria that professionals or experts evaluate in the relevant area (Chan & Chan, 2010; Saaty, 2008b). The pair-wise comparison can be carried out using Saaty's (1980a) 1–9 Likert scale (see Table 5.2). It breaks down difficult decisions into a sequence of one-to-one comparisons (Pair-wise comparisons) and synthesizes the results. AHP generally employs paired comparisons of objects that share a common goal or set of criteria. Paired groups are used to compare the principal criteria. Sub-criteria are also compared within. AHP makes use of the human ability to compare individual properties of alternatives. It assists decision-makers in selecting the best alternative and provides a clear justification for the selection.

It should be noted that in the AHP, all of the decision problems are regarded as having an ordered structure. In order of structure, the first level signifies the goal of a specific decision-making problem. While, in the second level, the goal is broken down into many criteria, the following levels can use the same principle to divide into further sub-criteria. AHP is an effective tool for dealing with complex decision-making and explaining how decision-makers use judgment when faced with complex, non-programmed decisions. AHP has been extensively employed in many fields to reflect the importance (weights) of the factors associated with priorities (Vaidya & Kumar, 2006). The primary goal of AHP is to classify many alternatives based on a given set of qualitative and quantitative criteria, using pair-wise comparison (judgment) provided by the decision-makers (Tsinidou et al., 2010). The AHP includes three primary operations: hierarchy construction, priority analysis, and consistency verification.

Firstly, decision-makers should divide complex multiple-criteria decision problems into hierarchical levels. The decision process's priority is followed by the following criteria, which can then be divided into sub-criteria. Lastly, the bottom level presents the alternatives to be considered (Ho et al., 2006). Furthermore, the AHP includes a valuable technique for examining the consistency of the decision-makers' evaluations to quantify the degree of consistency among pair-wise comparisons by calculating the consistency ratio, which is regarded as one of the AHP's

Table 5.2 The semantic scale for AHP

Importance	Definition	Description
1	Equally important	Elements/criteria A_i and A_j are equally important
3	A_j is more important than A_i	Experience and judgment are slightly favoring A_i over A_j
5	Essential or highly important	Experience and judgment strongly favoring A_i over A_j
7	Demonstrated the importance	A_i is very strongly favoring over A_j
9	Definitely importance	The evidence favoring A_i over A_j is of the highest possible order of affirmation
2, 4, 6, 8	Mediocre	When compromise is needed, values between two adjacent judgment are used
Reciprocals of the above judgments	If A_i has one of the above judgments assigned to it when compared with A_j, then A_j has the reciprocal value when compared with A_i	A reasonable assumption

Source Saaty (1980a)

most significant advantages (Lee et al., 2008). The consistency verification operation of AHP contributes significantly to preventing inconsistency by acting as a feedback mechanism for the decision-makers to evaluate and revise their judgments.

It is not easy to determine which objective is more important than the other and how it leads to the appropriate solution while working with complex problems with a possibility of many errors in making the trade-offs. A framework must be developed to address the issues in an organized manner to address this issue there. This type of framework is provided by AHP (Bayazit & Karpak, 2007).

Because a decision-maker bases his or her decision-making on knowledge and experience, the AHP approach is consistent with decision-making behavior (Al-Harbi, 2001). The evaluation was carried out by establishing pair-wise comparison judgments, which shaped a numeric depiction of each comparison in the form of a point estimate. The eigenvector method calculates priorities (or prioritize), and the linear additive value function is synthesized.

THE ANALYTICAL HIERARCHY PROCESS METHODOLOGY

The methodology used in this paper to perform AHP analysis is made into four sections. The first one describes the mathematical formulation of AHP, the second section illustrates the estimation procedure, the third section discusses factor/sub-factor identification/specifications and problem decomposition, and the fourth and final section describes the survey procedure, data, and software used.

FORMULATION OF AHP

AHP was proposed and developed by Saaty (1978), and it is a Multi-Criteria Decision-Making (MCDM) method. The basic assumption of any MCDM can be designed using a ranked method with various qualitative or quantitative judging criteria. The simplest one is to choose alternative subjects to a single layer of judging criteria. This is illustrated in Fig. 6.1 and shows that there are i alternatives to the problem, namely $A_1, A_2, \ldots, A_i$. Also, there are n judging criteria $C_1, C_2, \ldots, C_n$. One crucial step in AHP analysis is to conduct pair-wise comparisons between the criteria. Assume w_{ij} is such relative weighting of criterion i over criterion j, and that no interdependency exists among the criteria, the relative weighting of criterion j over criterion i then the pair-wise comparisons can be represented by questionnaires with subjective perceptions as:

$$A = \begin{bmatrix} a_{11} & \cdots & a_{1j} & \cdots & a_{1n} \\ \vdots & \ddots & \vdots & \ddots & \vdots \\ a_{i1} & \cdots & a_{ij} & \cdots & a_{in} \\ \vdots & \ddots & \vdots & \ddots & \vdots \\ a_{n1} & \cdots & a_{nj} & \cdots & a_{nm} \end{bmatrix} \quad (5.1)$$

where $a_{ij} = 1/a_{ji}$ (positive reciprocal) and $a_{ij} = a_{ik}/a_{jk}$. It should be noted that in practical times w_i/w_j is usually not known. So, the issue for the AHP is to find a_{ij} such that $a_{ij} \cong w_i/w_j$.

Let a weight matrix be represented as:

$$W = \begin{array}{c} w_1 \\ \vdots \\ w_i \\ \vdots \\ w_n \end{array} \begin{bmatrix} w_1/w_1 & \cdots & w_1/w_j & \cdots & w_1/w_n \\ \vdots & \ddots & \vdots & \ddots & \vdots \\ w_i/w_1 & \cdots & w_i/w_j & \cdots & w_i/w_n \\ \vdots & \ddots & \vdots & \ddots & \vdots \\ w_n/w_1 & \cdots & w_n/w_j & \cdots & w_n/w_n \end{bmatrix} \quad (5.2)$$

with column header $w_1 \cdots w_j \cdots w_n$

multiplying W by w yield

$$W \times w = \begin{array}{c} w_1 \\ \vdots \\ w_i \\ \vdots \\ w_n \end{array} \begin{bmatrix} w_1/w_1 & \cdots & w_1/w_j & \cdots & w_1/w_n \\ \vdots & \ddots & \vdots & \ddots & \vdots \\ w_i/w_1 & \cdots & w_i/w_j & \cdots & w_i/w_n \\ \vdots & \ddots & \vdots & \ddots & \vdots \\ w_n/w_1 & \cdots & w_n/w_j & \cdots & w_n/w_n \end{bmatrix} \begin{bmatrix} w_1 \\ \vdots \\ w_j \\ \vdots \\ w_n \end{bmatrix} = n \begin{bmatrix} w_1 \\ \vdots \\ w_j \\ \vdots \\ w_n \end{bmatrix}$$

(5.3)

Or

$$(W - nI)w = 0 \quad (5.4)$$

Table 5.2 denotes the ratio scale used to compare the weight between criteria according to the linguistic meaning from 1 to 9 (Saaty & Kearns, 1991; Saaty, 1980a, 1985, 1990) to represent an equal significance extremely significant.

Solving Eq. 5.4 is the problem of eigenvalue. The relative weights can be derived by finding the eigenvector w with respective λ_{max} that satisfies $Aw = \lambda_{max}$ the average eigenvalue of the matrix A, i.e., find the eigenvector w with respective λ_{max} for $(A - \lambda_{max}I)w = 0$. Furthermore, two indices, including the Consistency Index (CI) and the Consistency Ratio (CR), are recommended to ensure the consistency of the subjective perception and the relative weights' accuracy. The CI equation can be expressed as:

$$\text{CI} = (\lambda_{max} - n)/(n-1) \Rightarrow w = (w_1, w_2, \ldots, w_n) \quad (5.5)$$

Table 5.3 The random consistency index (RI) for different matrix sizes

N	2	3	4	5	6	7	8	9	10	11	12	13
RI	0.00	0.52	0.89	1.11	1.25	1.35	1.4	1.45	1.49	1.51	1.54	1.56

Source Saaty (1980a)

where λ_{max} is the highest eigenvalue, and the number of attributes is denoted by n. Saaty (1980a) suggested that CR's value should not exceed 0.1 for a confident result. On the other hand, the CR can be calculated as:

$$CR = \frac{CI}{RI} \quad (5.6)$$

RI denotes a random consistency index derived from a large sample of randomly generated reciprocal matrices using the scale $1/9, 1/8, ..., 1, ..., 8, 9$. The RI concerning different size matrices is shown in Table 5.3. The C.R. should be under 0.1 for a reliable result (Saaty, 1980a), and 0.2 is the maximum tolerated (Tzeng & Huang, 2011) level.

Estimation Procedures:

The AHP allows the problem to be decomposed down to a hierarchy of subsequent problems that can, in turn, be more easily understood and evaluated. The evaluations are converted into numerical values, then used to rank each alternative on a numerical scale. The AHP method can be explained in the study's following steps:

Saaty (1980a, 1985, 1990) and Saaty and Kearns (1991) put together the following steps for applying the AHP:

1. Setting goals based on the problems determined.
2. A step level with the primary objectives with the highest priority, which shall be followed by intermediary levels and ends with the last level with a list of alternatives
3. Establishing sets with the comparison matrices (size $n \times n$) for every lower level with matrix for every component in a level directly above it using the relative scale measurement shown in Table 5.2. The pairwise comparisons are made in terms of which component dominates the other.

4. The $n(n-1)$/judgments are essential to make matrices in the 3rd step. Reciprocals are usually automatically allocated in each pair-wise comparison.
5. The hierarchical combination is then employed to weigh the eigenvectors by the weights of the criteria. The sum is taken over all weighted eigenvector entries matching those in the next lower hierarchy level.
6. After all the pair-wise judgments are made, the consistency is drawn out using the eigenvalue λ_{max} to compute the consistency index, CI as follows: CI = $(\lambda_{max} - n)/(n - 1)$, where n is the matrix size. Judgment consistency can be cross-checked by taking the consistency ratio (CR) of CI with the suitable value of RI in Table 5.3. The CR (CR = CI/RI) is satisfactory if not exceeding 0.10 (Saaty, 1980a). If it is more, the judgment matrix is inconsistent. To get a consistent matrix, judgments have to be reviewed and improvised.
7. Steps 3–6 are executed for all of the levels in the hierarchy.

Factor/Sub-factor and Strategy, Sub-strategy Identification/Specification: Factors/sub-factors and strategies/sub-strategies are reported separately because the prioritization is performed for two distinct goals (i.e., consumers' preferences and retailers' counter-strategies prioritization).

i. Factors/Sub-factors Identification for Consumer Preferences in Organized Retailing

The nine factors and 32 sub-factors of consumer preferences in organized retailing are identified, validated, and demonstrated through EFA and CFA. Therefore, in this section, directly, the factors and sub-factors of consumer preferences are only cited. Table 5.4 depicts the nine consumer preference factors and 32 sub-factors. Table 5.5 gives the definitions of the consumer preference factors used in the study.

ii. Retailers' Strategies/Sub-strategies Identification for Addressing Consumer Preferences in Organized Retailing

It is far more critical for any retailer to define counter-strategies to meet consumer preferences and expectations than to identify consumers'

Table 5.4 Factors and sub-factors of consumer preferences in organized retailing

Factors/criteria	Sub-factors/sub-criteria
Store atmospherics	Ambiance
	Aesthetics
	Cleanliness
	Store facilities
Pricing & value	Value for money
	Discounts & offers
	Affordability
	Loyalty rewards as cash discount/special offers
Assortment	Availability/never stock-out
	Latest & trendy products
	Attractive display/placement
In-store delights	Touch & feel/in-store trail
	Fast & easy billing/POS & checkout
	In-store digitization
	Customer consultancy
Convenience	One-stop shopping
	Large/spacious store with proper layout & signage
	Location (Prime market area)
Product/service quality & reliability	High-quality branded products
	Reliable and high-quality service(s)
	Reliable information sharing (about latest offerings)
Person-to-person experience	Highly responsive/prompt service
	Empathy/politeness in employees' behavior
	Informative Employees with good knowledge of offerings
	Individual customer attention
Problem-solving	Prompt handling of customer complaint & queries

(continued)

Table 5.4 (continued)

Factors/criteria	Sub-factors/sub-criteria
Entertainment	Listening to VOC/Suggestions/Feedbacks Hassle-free return & exchange Guarantee/warranty Recreation/hangout Food zone Movies/shows or events

Source Extracted and validated from both literature review further validated by experts in a pilot study

preferred factors. As a result, this section identifies highly relevant strategies and sub-strategies concerning consumers' preferred factors and sub-factors through interpretive expert mining to provide retailers with prioritized strategies for addressing consumers' preferences. According to the name of the newly adopted method (Interpretive AHP—iAHP), the first step entails meticulously identifying and listing the strategies and sub-strategies about the consumer preference construct. Experts in academia (faculty members and researchers in marketing/retailing) and experts from the relevant sector, namely organized retailing (store managers/customer relation managers and shop floor executives), were consulted for this purpose. The experts were asked to specify the most relevant strategy and sub-strategy/steps that organized retailers adopt/implement to respond to consumers' preferential expectations (as mentioned in Table 5.4. After several meetings and interpretive discussion sessions (in-person/over the phone/email) with the experts, the most relevant strategy and sub-strategy were explored (Table 5.6), and a description of the explored strategies and sub-strategies is furnished in Table 5.7 to prioritize the same using AHP (logically named as *i*AHP). However, no mathematical or procedural modifications have been made to the *i*AHP, and it is the same as the AHP methodology. The only new aspect is exploring strategies via interpretive expert mining (the identified and validated consumer preference scale in this study). Because the expert mining process was performed directly with organized retail store managers and experts such as researchers/Professors in the relevant domain, the interpretive strategy exploration technique minimizes ambiguity regarding the explored strategy/sub-strategies.

Table 5.5 Definitions of the dimension and judgments used in the study (consumer perspective)

Sl. No.	Factors	Definition/description
F1	Store atmospherics	The atmospherics of a store is the generic characteristics a physical store is given to attract the potential customer to that retail space and give a feel of enticing to the customers to participate in the shopping activity. The store's atmospherics are usually designed to increase customer experience while shopping and influence their mood
F2	Pricing & value	Retailer's pricing strategy that the consumers perceive as s/he is getting the optimum value for the amount spent on a particular product or service. This factor is one of the most valued factors for supermarket store shoppers (of Odisha) as they are price sensitive
F3	Assortment	The different types of products and services a business offers are the product assortment. Modern-day large-format retailers are popularly known for maintaining a deep assortment (wide variety), attracting more customers
F4	In-store delights	It is the product/outcome of the interaction between the inside establishment of retail space and a customer throughout their relationship, which customers love to experience and get delighted
F5	Convenience	Convenience is the most critical aspect for many customers and marketers. Usually, any attempt which can effectively improve the convenience to the customers has always got instant appreciation. In particular, millennials are observed to be more convenience-oriented
F6	Product/service quality & reliability	Organized retail store customers wish to get better quality and reliable product/service from the store they visit for shopping. The degree to which these expectations are met is essential
F7	Person-to-person experience	Person-to-Person experience in large organized retail stores is directly associated with the core product. The more the staff at supermarkets are friendly the more customer would like to go shopping there. The staff's professionalism and friendliness are paramount
F8	Problem-solving	Problem-solving skills are essential for large-format retailers. Steps were taken to solve each customer query/complaint need serious attention of organized retailers as this is one of the bases of customers' evaluation of the satisfactory experience

(continued)

Table 5.5 (continued)

Sl. No.	Factors	Definition/description
F9	Entertainment	The modern way of merging shopping and *entertainment* opportunities as an anchor for customers in modern retail formats can attract more footfall as the shoppers prefer it

RESEARCH DESIGN AND METHODOLOGY

From the procedure above for AHP, the following stepladder was derived from performing AHP & *i*AHP for the defined goals (i.e., consumers' preferences and retailers' counter-strategies).

  i. Define the objective or goals
 ii. Decompose the objectives into sub-criteria
iii. Construction of hierarchy frameworks for analysis
 iv. Collection of empirical information and data
  v. Perform pair-wise comparisons for each level of criteria and sub-criteria
 vi. Check the consistency in the pair-wise comparison
vii. Calculate the global weights of each criterion and sub-criteria

To investigate the relative priorities of the consumers' preferred attributes in organized retailing and retailers' counter-strategies to address those preferences, data analysis was carried out in *seven steps*, as explained below in detail.

  i. Define the Goal

The goal was to prioritize consumers' preferred attributes in organized retailing and retailers' counter-strategies for addressing consumer preferences.

 ii. Decomposing the Objective into Sub-Criteria

The two objectives were decomposed into nine dimensions (Criteria) and 32 subsequent criteria each in this step. Factor extraction was carried

Table 5.6 Interpreted strategy and sub-strategies vis-à-vis consumers' preferred factors and sub-factors

Strategy/criteria	Sub-strategies/sub-criteria
Store atmosphere rejuvenation	Architecture revival
	Interior design
	Swachh drives (Littering free environment)
	Differentiated store facilities
Value-augmented pricing	Value (based) retailing
	Shopping hour-specific discounts & offers
	Rational pricing
	Direct cash discount
Merchandise management	Inventory/stock optimization
	Latest trend analytics and management
	Visual merchandising
Customer experience Management	Dedicated product experience zone/facility
	Convenient POS/billing & checkout
	Digital information sharing & Experience (In-Store digitization)
	Dedicated customer consultancy
Ease of accessibility	Everything under one roof
	Space planning & management
	Location planning & management
Quality management practices	Quality & brand management
	Service quality enhancement
	Trustworthy communication
Customer interaction augmentation	Response time minimization
	Employee grooming/behavioral excellence
	Employee orientation & knowledge up-gradation
	Customer touch-point attention
Grievance handling & management	Social response strategy
	VOC management through community development
	No question asked return/exchange policy
	Customer assurance building

(continued)

Table 5.6 (continued)

Strategy/criteria	Sub-strategies/sub-criteria
Retail-tainment (Socialization)	Consumer socialization Cafeteria/food zone (development & promotion) Event-based crowd-sourcing

Source Derived/Explored through Expert Mining vis-à-vis Consumer Preference Scale

out and validated for consumer preferences in organized retailing for the first objective (i.e., priorities of the consumers' preferred attributes in organized retailing). Based on that result, the problem's hierarchical abstraction was formed. For the first objective, the dimension categories (Criteria) considered were: store atmospherics, pricing and value, assortment, in-store delights, convenience, product/service quality and reliability, person-to-person experience, problem-solving, and entertainment. The sub-criteria identified for each main criteria were—ambience, aesthetics, cleanliness, store facilities, value for money, discount and offers, affordability, loyalty rewards as cash discount/special offers, availability/never stock-out, latest and trendy products, attractive display/placement, touch and feel/in-store trail, easy billing/POS and checkout, in-store digitization, customer consultancy, one-stop shopping, large/spacious store with proper layout and signage, location (prime market area), high-quality branded products, reliable and high-quality service(s), reliable information sharing (about all offerings), highly responsive/prompt service, empathy/politeness in employees' behavior, informative employees with good knowledge on offerings, individual customer intention, prompt handling of customer complaint and queries, listening to VOC/suggestions/feedbacks, hassle-free return and exchange, guarantee/warranty, recreation/hangout, cafeteria/Food zone (development and promotion) and movies/shows or events.

Similarly, expert mining was used to explore the criteria and sub-criteria for the second objective, prioritizing retailers' counter-strategies. Based on that result, the problem's hierarchical abstraction was formed. For the first objective, the dimension categories (Criteria) considered were: store atmosphere rejuvenation, value-augmented pricing, merchandise management, customer experience management, ease of accessibility, quality management practices, customer interaction augmentation,

Table 5.7 Definitions of the dimension and judgments used in the study (retailer perspective)

C_i	Brief description of confirmed construct (factors/criteria and sub-factor/sub-criteria)
C_1	**Store atmosphere rejuvenation**: Restructuring and giving an attractive/alluring look to the "Store Atmospherics" to a retail shop that entices customers to come to the store, designed to influence the customer's mood to increase the pleasure of their purchase being made. It characterizes the consumers' tendency to be attracted toward the particular store, which possesses alluring atmospherics (Chebat et al., 2014)
C_{11}	*Architecture revival*: Enhancing the character and atmosphere of a supermarket store and mall attracts consumers for a visit
C_{12}	*Interior design*: Attractive interior decoration of supermarket stores, which consumers akin to enjoy during their shopping. It could include the furniture, flooring, and music
C_{13}	*Swachh drives*: Keeping the store environment clean and littering free by regular *swachh* drives with the help of their staff at modern-day retail stores from which customers get a pleasant feeling and get attracted
C_{14}	*Differentiated store facilities*: Providing extra facilities at modern large-format retail stores that other stores do not provide or do not have such facilities [like drinking water, separate clean gents & ladies toilets, lift/escalator, seating area inside the store (couch/sofa) & outside store (canopy)]
C_2	**Value-augmented pricing**: Any product/offering by a retailer that is such priced that consumers feel it worth both physical attributes and the non-physical attributes against the money spent on that. Retailer's pricing strategy that the consumers perceive as s/he is getting the optimum value for the amount spent on a product or a service
C_{21}	*Value-based retailing*: Value-based retailing is a pricing strategy adopted by retailers that set prices primarily, but not exclusively, according to the perceived or estimated value of a product or service to the customer rather than according to the cost of the product or historical prices

C_i	Brief description of confirmed construct (factors/criteria and sub-factor/sub-criteria)
C_{22}	**Shopping hour-specific discounts & offers**: a deduction from the full amount of a price to promote prompt purchases during specific shopping hours (specifically during odd hours when customer footfall is low) to surprise customers and boost sales (Jin & Kim, 2003)
C_{23}	**Rational pricing**: Pricing strategy based on or following reason or logic that the cost or price of something that retailers offer is affordable. Consumers show their ability to afford the same (Hoffman et al., 2002; Lal & Matutes, 1994)
C_{24}	**Direct cash discount**: Money or any direct discount offered to customers and enticed potential customers to choose a particular retail outlet for their repeat purchase(s)
C_3	**Merchandise management**: Merchandising is the information regarding the variety of products and services available with the seller in a store. The management of merchandise is a visual apprehends of displaying those products and services
C_{31}	**Inventory/stock balancing**: Inventory optimization in retailing is a way to balance the capital investment constraints and service-level goals in stock-keeping units (SKUs) while taking demand and supply volatility into account. The wide variety of products that supermarket stores maintain reassures consumers that the products they are looking for will never be out of stock at the supermarket stores/malls (Fisher et al., 2001; Smith & Agrawal, 2000)
C_{32}	**Latest trend analytics & management**: The rampant practice of collecting information and attempting to spot a pattern by analyzing the *modern* and most *recent* fashions or ideas that modern consumers are motivated with for their shopping (Finn & Louviere, 1996)

(continued)

Table 5.7 (continued)

C_i	Brief description of confirmed construct (factors/criteria and sub-factor/sub-criteria)
C_{33}	*Visual merchandising*: The presentation of the store's products in an attempt to attract the attention of a consumer is what visual merchandising is mostly about. From the store's decoration to the music played in the store, all are a part of it
C_4	**Customer experience management**: A retailer is always interested in gathering the customer's experience; they track and learn the interaction between a customer and the retailer throughout the customer lifecycle (Grewal et al., 2009; Kamaladevi, 2010)
C_{41}	*Dedicated experience zone/facilities*: A premise inside retail stores (on every floor in case of multi-storied shopping centers) intended to provide direct experience by allowing consumers to examine, use or test a product before their purchase
C_{42}	*Convenient POS/billing/Checkout*: The retail transaction place must be highly convenient. Getting the products billed at the retail store's counter and letting them move out of the store with their purchase without hassle (Seiders et al., 2000)
C_{43}	*Digital information sharing & experience*: Providing information to the consumers through a digital medium by retailers, including digital information sharing through big digital screens, audiovisual aids, smartphone app, Wi-Fi, & NFC (Near Field Communication)
C_{44}	*Dedicated customer consultancy*: Dedicated providing first-hand information and assistance regarding any product/offering or usage-related queries at the retailer's premises (Solomon, 1987)

C_i	Brief description of confirmed construct (factors/criteria and sub-factor/sub-criteria)
C_5	**Ease of accessibility**: The degree of ease of availability of a good or service to the customer is the ease of accessibility
C_{51}	*Everything under one roof*: A retail location that offers many offerings to customers in one place (Srivastava, 2008)
C_{52}	*Space planning & management*: the placing of products in the store is a strategic phenomenon. Space has to be planned to efficiently adjust the presentation of the products in the store, which can attract the customer efficiently
C_{53}	*Location planning & management*: A retail outlet situated in a city/town is a strategic advantage for retailers (Berman et al., 1995). Many factors like reachability, parking convenience, etc., draw the consumers
C_6	**Quality management practices**: Quality Management practices in retailing ensure that a retailer is a consistent product/service/offerings
C_{61}	*Quality & brand management*: Brand management in retailing analyzes and plans how the store's maintained brands are perceived in the market and how the local shoppers perceive its quality aspect (Porter & Claycomb, 1997)
C_{62}	*Service quality enhancement*: When a perceived expectation (E) of a service is compared by perceived performance (P), it gives service quality. The retailers strive to minimization of the PE gap. Retailers can perform the promised service dependably and accurately (Dabholkar, 1995)
C_{63}	*Reliable communication*: Exchange of highly reliable facts and figures on offerings by retailers to customers
C_7	**Customer interaction augmentation**: Personal responses to the customers align with the consumer expectation either directly or indirectly at every touch-point. Person-to-Person interaction experience in large organized retail stores is directly affiliated to customer satisfaction (Nurhayati & Hendar, 2017)

(continued)

Table 5.7 (continued)

C_i	Brief description of confirmed construct (factors/criteria and sub-factor/sub-criteria)
	C_{71} *Response time minimization*: Minimizing the time elapsed between the customer's requesting of products till they receive the receipts of them. The speed process can be in terms of checkout counters, opening hours, and queue at counters
	C_{72} *Employee grooming/behavioral excellence*: Enhancing the retail store employees' ability to understand and share customers' feelings. Organized retail store customers seek empathy/politeness from employees, and if not received, this hurts customers' assessments of retailers' service quality (Jha & Mahmoud, 2017; Lindblom et al., 2016)
	C_{73} *Employee orientation & knowledge up-gradation*: Retail store employees' store-related knowledge up-gradation through regular employee orientation and sharing information regarding each offering proves to be advantageous for retailers. When employees are knowledgeable, capable, and efficient, they can keep customers happy and loyal (Reed et al., 2016)
	C_{74} *Customer touch-point attention*: When retailers interact with customers at any touch-point, it is necessary to provide the personal attention customers deserve (Grewal et al., 2009; Stein & Ramaseshan, 2016)
C_8	**Grievance handling & management**: Any dissatisfaction or feeling of injustice connected with a customer's purchase brought to the attention of retail store management and steps taken to solve the same. Each customer query/complaint need the profound attention of organized retailers (Gilly & Hansen, 1985)
	C_{81} *Social response strategy*: Response to customer complaints and queries through websites, email, social media platforms, and mass information dissemination with the help of customer/household information captured from loyalty, website, or social data (Grewal et al., 2017)
	C_{82} *VOC management through community development*: Creating and implementing needs assessment surveys of local shoppers, taking into account the customer feedbacks, listening to the voice of the customers, and providing improved services by engaging local stakeholders in visioning sessions
	C_{83} *No question asked exchange/return policy*: An optimal return policy and hassle-free offering of an exchange or a return to the customer in case of post-purchase dissatisfaction (Shang et al., 2017)

C_i	Brief description of confirmed construct (factors/criteria and sub-factor/sub-criteria)
C_{84}	**Customer assurance building**: Building assurance among customers regarding their spending on every purchase (typically in writing, maybe in the form of a bill) that certain conditions will be fulfilled, especially that a product will be repaired or replaced if not of a specified quality (Ahsan & Rahman, 2016)
C_9	**Retail-tainment (Socialization)**: Retail-tainment is the concept of adding entertainment and experiences to the retail mix. The modern trend of combining shopping and entertainment opportunities as an anchor for customers in modern retail formats can attract more footfall as the shoppers prefer it (White, 2010)
C_{91}	**Consumer socialization**: The "collective processes by which young people acquire skills, knowledge, and attitudes relevant to their functioning as consumers in the marketplace" (Ward, 1974). Such a process may influence modern young recreational consumers during their visits to shopping centers and malls (Kim & Kim, 2016)
C_{92}	**Cafeteria/Food Zone (Development & promotion)**: Developing cafeteria/food zone inside the premises or adjacent to modern retail outlets to attract customers with diverse interests
C_{93}	**Event-based crowd-sourcing**: Organization of fashion shows and entertainment events and built-in movie theaters at modern shopping centers/shopping malls for customer attraction (Kohler & Nickel, 2017)

grievance handling and management, and retailtainment/socialization. The sub-strategies explored for each strategies through expert mining were—architecture revival, interior design, swachh drives (littering free environment), value (based) retailing, shopping hour-specific discounts and offers, rational pricing, direct cash discount, inventory/stock optimization, latest trend analytics and management, visual merchandizing, dedicated product experience zone/facility, convenient POS/billing and checkout, digital information sharing and experience (store digitization), dedicated customer consultancy, everything under one roof, space planning and management, location planning and management, product quality and brand management, service quality enhancement, trustworthy communication, response time minimization, employee grooming/behavioral excellence, employee orientation and knowledge up-gradation, customer touch-point attention, social response strategy, VOC management through community development, no question asked return/exchange policy, customer assurance building, consumer socialization, cafeteria/food zone (development and promotion) and event-based crowd-sourcing.

iii. Construction of Hierarchy Framework for Analysis

At this stage, two hierarchy frameworks were built. The first was for the consumer preference goal, and the second was for the retailer's strategic goal. Steps 1 and 2 were used to identify relevant and essential criteria and sub-criteria of the strategy for "consumer preference" and the retailer's strategy after the goal of the strategy for "consumer preference" and the retailer's strategy was established. The descending hierarchical structures were designed with the overall objective and goals for each stage in mind. Using the guidelines proposed by (Saaty, 2001) for hierarchy structure, the AHP framework has developed both goals for facilitating the study.

Figures 5.2 and 5.3 show a multi-level decision hierarchy, including these criteria and the subsequent ones. The first step in the AHP is to build the decision problem's hierarchy. There are no hard and fast rules for making the hierarchy. This making gives a difficult choice to be prearranged into the system resulting from an objective to different criteria, following criteria until the lowest level is reached. The prominent principle followed was contemplating the complex problem, listing all of the crucial ideas, variables, and alternatives, and then reorganizing them in a hierarchy that compares the elements of lower levels with the following higher-level elements. According to Saaty (1990), the human mind innovatively displays its abilities by dividing a problem into essential elements like goals, criteria, and alternatives. Following this procedure, a large amount of information can be put together to form a picture of the complete system from the structure of the problem.

The cream of the hierarchy represents the objectives or goals of the decisions. At the middle levels, the criteria and the following criteria that influence decisions are represented. Finally, at the last level of the hierarchy, the alternatives or options are laid out. According to Saaty (2001), building a hierarchy through artistic thinking, memory, and perspectives is possible. He also mentions the lack of a set of procedures for creating

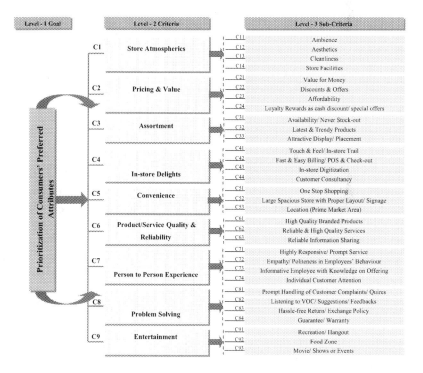

Fig. 5.2 Goal, criteria, and sub-criteria of consumer preference hierarchy (*Source* Developed by authors)

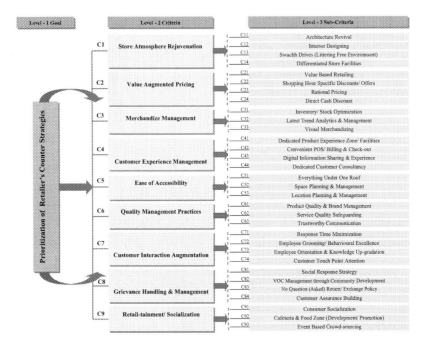

Fig. 5.3 Goal, criteria, and sub-criteria of retailers' strategy hierarchy (*Source* Developed by authors)

the levels comprised in the hierarchy. According to (Bayazit & Karpak, 2007), the hierarchy structure is decided by the nature of decisions at the managerial level. In addition, the number of layers in the hierarchy is decided by the complications in the problem which is being analyzed and the level of detail required by an analyst to solve the problem. As a result, the hierarchical depiction of a system may differ from person to person. This analysis seeks to identify indicators relevant to two distinct aspects of organized retailing: consumer preferences and retailers' counter-strategies to address those preferences.

iv. Survey Procedure (Collection of empirical information and data)

Two separate questionnaires were developed to collect pair-wise comparison data from both consumers' and retailers'/experts' perspectives, according to the study's requirements and the procedure laid out by Saaty (1980a, 1985, 1990) and Saaty and Kearns (1991) to carry out AHP. The first part of the AHP questionnaire was its main element, providing a pair-wise assessment of the nine dimensions in each case; then, the sub-criteria of the nine dimensions, and finally, the demographic characteristics of the evaluators/experts. The first sub-section of the first questionnaire deals with store atmosphere (four sub-factors). The second sub-section is about pricing and value (four sub-factors). The third sub-section is concerned with the assortment (three sub-factors). The fourth sub-section is about in-store treats (four sub-factors). The fifth sub-section is concerned with convenience (three sub-factors). The sixth sub-section is concerned with product/service quality and dependability (three sub-factors). The seventh sub-section is concerned with the person-to-person experience (four sub-factors). The eighth sub-section is concerned with problem-solving (four sub-factors). The ninth and final sub-section is about entertainment (three sub-factors). The second section includes the necessary information about respondents, such as their location and position. The authors interviewed five experts (three of whom are marketing/retail faculty members, and the other two are store managers) to confirm the AHP questionnaire's reliability and validity. The wording and structure of the AHP questionnaires were slightly changed as a result of those interviews. The entire questionnaire for both survey phases was distributed in person and via email. To avoid confusion, experts were contacted both personally and over the phone. Before proceeding with the survey, it was critical to finalize the size of the evaluator/expert groups in both cases. The size of the group influences the efficiency of group decision-making; it is recommended that 5–20 experts participate in the validation. As a result, the size of the decision-making group should be kept to a minimum; it should be between 5 and 50 people (Gumus, 2009).

As mentioned earlier in this paper, two different surveys were conducted for data collection. Data was collected from individual evaluators in the first survey, i.e., heavy supermarket shoppers. A careful approach was followed to choose evaluators/experts. Those shoppers were chosen to spend quite a hefty amount (>5000) in almost every store visit. The heavy shoppers were identified based on purchase history-based loyalty card data. The supermarket store managers in the four cities of India, i.e., *Delhi, Mumbai, Kolkata, and Chennai,* were approached for contact details of heavy and loyal shoppers with a self-declaration and a recommendation letter (from the thesis supervisor) cum undertaking that the information of heavy shoppers and the data collected from them shall be kept confidential and shall solely be used for academic research work. The four cities were selected based on geographical location (one city from the east, west, north, and south region of India). Some of the retailers were reluctant to disclose such information about their customers. However, as the sample size required to perform AHP is relatively minor, contacting the heavy and loyal shoppers is considered experts in this study phase. In the present study, 40 evaluators/experts[1] were approached to participate. However, 35 experts (heavy shoppers) finally participated in the research, and out of them, only 27 gave a complete response to the questionnaire (Appendix III). The response rate was slightly low (as 27 complete questionnaires were received back), with a response rate of 67.5%. The detailed demographic profile of evaluators is given in Table 5.8.

Similarly, academic and industry experts (from the organized retail sector) were contacted for the second survey. Faculty and research scholars in marketing/retailing and store managers, customer relationship managers, and shop floor executives were approached to provide feedback on a pair-wise comparative scale questionnaire (Appendix IV) developed based on strategies and sub-strategies identified through accurate interpretation and expert mining. A total of ten faculty members, eleven research scholars from state universities, and fourteen store managers/ customer relation managers/shop floor executives from three randomly selected stores in each of the four cities were approached for the survey, and 23 agreed to participate. Finally, for further analysis, a total of 16 complete and valid responses (with a response rate of 69.56 percent) are considered. Table 5.9 depicts the demographic profile of the experts.

Their experience and expertise in this field aid in determining the criteria and the sub-criteria and their respective importance of the study's objectives (Talib et al., 2011). Two different questionnaires were used to generate the responses. The prejudice of decisions is a realistic result of the decision-system maker's appropriate values; however, according to Bayazit

---

[1] Randomly 10 most loyal shoppers from the contact details provided by all supermarket store managers (only those who were willing to provide) in each city were contacted to collect the pair-wise comparative data.

Table 5.8 Evaluators' profile[2] (Group 1: heavy and loyal customers)

Gender	
Male	16
Female	11
Age	
26–35	8
36–45	11
46–55	5
56 or above	3
Marital status	
Married	17
Unmarried	10
Education level	
Graduate	9
Post Graduate	13
PhD	2
Others	3
Occupation	
Employed	15
Self-employed	9
Unemployed	3
Shopping experience	
Less than a year	4
1–2 years	5
3–4 years	10
5 Years and above	8
Location	
Bhubaneswar	7
Sambalpur	6
Baripada	6
Berhampur	8

and Karpak (2007), whether consciously or unconsciously, the evaluation matrix based on decisions does not depend on the decision-makers' characteristics. It has to be emphasized that the expert group size was small, but previous research has shown that AHP analysis can be used with as few as a few respondents. In a few studies, as few as two respondents/experts were used (Saaty, 1980a, 2008b). The researcher personally collected the data, ensuring proper responses and avoiding invalid responses. The

---

[2] To maintain confidentiality, the name and location details of the evaluators/experts are not disclosed. However, it may be revealed on written request through proper channel.

Table 5.9 Experts' profile[3] (Group 2: Academic & retail industry experts)

Gender	
Male	9
Female	7
Age	
26–35	4
36–45	6
46–55	4
56 or above	2
Marital status	
Married	7
Unmarried	9
Education level	
Graduate	5
Post Graduate	7
PhD	4
Others	0
Occupation	
Employed	13
Unemployed	3
Designation	
Reader/professors (academics)	4
Research scholars	4
SM/ASM/CRM[a]	4
Shop floor executives	4
Shopping experience	
Less than 3 year	6
4–6 years	3
7–9 years	3
10 Years or above	4
Location	
Bhubaneswar	4
Sambalpur	4
Baripada	4
Berhampur	4

[a] *SM* Store Managers, *ASM* Assistant Store Managers, *CRM* Customer Relation Managers disclose

experts/respondents were given specific instructions and encouraged to seek clarification if they had any questions.

After determining the size and composition of the expert group, the survey was launched. The first questionnaire was developed based on

---

[3] To maintain confidentiality, the name and location details of the experts are not disclosed. However, it may be revealed on written request through proper channel.

consumer preference factors and sub-factors validated through EFA and CFA from the consumers' perspective. Following "expert mining," the second questionnaire for the retailers'/experts' prospective study was developed. To prioritize retailers' counter-strategies for consumer preferences, expert mining was used to extract organized retailers' in-practice counter-strategies to confront consumer preferences. Retailers' in-practice counter-strategies and sub-strategies were extracted and listed after a thorough interpretation of consumers' preferred factors and subsequent factors. As a result, the pair-wise comparison method was used to finalize the second questionnaire for retail store managers/experts.

Empirical Analysis

After gathering the data, the following step evaluated the relative significance of the criteria and the following criteria at every level. As a result, the AHP approach was employed to compute the importance using pair-wise comparisons, and outcomes were organized in a matrix format. In both cases, evaluators/experts were asked to carefully compare every hierarchy level criterion by assigning a relative scale in a pair-wise (Saaty, 2008b) fashion to both models' goals or objectives. In both cases, the experts were invited to rate a pair-wise comparison of nine dimensions and related 32 variables (Sub-Criteria). Paired comparisons were made for each group on a fundamental scale of 1–9 (Chen, 2004; Saaty, 1980a, 1985, 1990, 2008b), which indicates the various degrees of relative importance (refer to Table 5.2).

Based on the results of the pair-wise comparison (Saaty, 2008b) of the evaluators/experts in both surveys, the scores of each evaluator/expert were entered into a comparison matrix (1–9 scale). The ratings/individual judgments of all evaluators/experts were then aggregated using Saaty's (1990) geometric mean, and average matrices were prepared for further analysis. A similar procedure was followed for the sub-criteria, and all of the average matrices for both cases are provided separately below.

The *first expert group* was the heavy and loyal shoppers who were taken as experts to rate their priorities by following the paired comparison method prescribed by Saaty (1980a, 1985, 1990, 2008b). Each "heavy shopper," where $p = 1, 2, 3, ..., 27$ individually carried out pair-wise evaluation using Saaty's 1–9 scale for the nine factors/criteria and 32 sub-factors/sub-criteria of consumer preferences related to organized retailing.

The collected information was then summarized by computing the average values of all 27 responses of experts (heavy and loyal shoppers) from the selected four cities in Odisha, and the final matrix obtained for further calculation/analysis is as follows:

a. Average matrix for nine consumer preference factors
$c_1\ c_2\ c_3\ c_4\ c_5\ c_6\ c_7\ c_8\ c_9$

$$H_1 = \begin{array}{c} c_1 \\ c_2 \\ c_3 \\ c_4 \\ c_5 \\ c_6 \\ c_7 \\ c_8 \\ c_9 \end{array} \begin{bmatrix} 1 & 1/2 & 1/5 & 1/7 & 5 & 3 & 7 & 2 & 1 \\ 2 & 1 & 1 & 1 & 7 & 7 & 9 & 9 & 5 \\ 5 & 1 & 1 & 1 & 7 & 3 & 7 & 7 & 3 \\ 7 & 1 & 1 & 1 & 9 & 9 & 7 & 7 & 9 \\ 1/5 & 1/7 & 1/7 & 1/9 & 1 & 1/5 & 1 & 2 & 3 \\ 1/3 & 1/7 & 1/3 & 1/9 & 5 & 1 & 5 & 3 & 1/3 \\ 1/7 & 1/9 & 1/7 & 1/7 & 1 & 1/5 & 1 & 3 & 1/7 \\ 1/2 & 1/9 & 1/7 & 1/7 & 2 & 1/3 & 1/3 & 1 & 1/2 \\ 1 & 1/5 & 1/3 & 1/9 & 3 & 3 & 7 & 2 & 1 \end{bmatrix}$$

In the same way, the pair-wise comparison (Saaty, 2008b) matrices for all 32 sub-factors under the nine factors (as follows) were prepared for further analysis.

b. Average matrix for first consumer preference sub-factor: Store Atmospherics
$c_1\ c_2\ c_3\ c_4$

$$H_{1,1} = \begin{array}{c} c_1 \\ c_2 \\ c_3 \\ c_4 \end{array} \begin{bmatrix} 1 & 3 & 5 & 1/2 \\ 1/3 & 1 & 2 & 1/7 \\ 1/5 & 1/2 & 1 & 1/5 \\ 2 & 7 & 5 & 1 \end{bmatrix}$$

c. Average matrix for second consumer preference sub-factor: Pricing & Value
$c_1\ c_2\ c_3\ c_4$

$$H_{1,2} = \begin{array}{c} c_1 \\ c_2 \\ c_3 \\ c_4 \end{array} \begin{bmatrix} 1 & 5 & 7 & 2 \\ 1/5 & 1 & 3 & 1 \\ 1/7 & 1/3 & 1 & 1/3 \\ 1/2 & 1 & 3 & 1 \end{bmatrix}$$

d. Average matrix for third consumer preference sub-factor: Assortment

$c_1\ c_2\ c_3$

$$H_{1.3} = \begin{matrix} c_1 \\ c_2 \\ c_3 \end{matrix} \begin{bmatrix} 1 & 1/9 & 1/5 \\ 9 & 1 & 3 \\ 5 & 1/3 & 1 \end{bmatrix}$$

e. Average matrix for fourth consumer preference sub-factor: In-store Delights

$c_1\ c_2\ c_3\ c_4$

$$H_{1.4} = \begin{matrix} c_1 \\ c_2 \\ c_3 \\ c_4 \end{matrix} \begin{bmatrix} 1 & 1/2 & 2 & 1 \\ 2 & 1 & 4 & 5 \\ 1/2 & 1/4 & 1 & 1 \\ 1 & 1/5 & 1 & 1 \end{bmatrix}$$

f. Average matrix for fifth consumer preference sub-factor: Convenience

$c_1\ c_2\ c_3$

$$H_{1.5} = \begin{matrix} c_1 \\ c_2 \\ c_3 \end{matrix} \begin{bmatrix} 1 & 1 & 9 \\ 1 & 1 & 5 \\ 1/9 & 1/5 & 1 \end{bmatrix}$$

g. Average matrix for sixth consumer preference sub-factor: Product/Service Quality & Reliability

$c_1\ c_2\ c_3$

$$H_{1.6} = \begin{matrix} c_1 \\ c_2 \\ c_3 \end{matrix} \begin{bmatrix} 1 & 1 & 7 \\ 1 & 1 & 5 \\ 1/7 & 1/5 & 1 \end{bmatrix}$$

h. Average matrix for seventh consumer preference sub-factor: Person-to-Person Experience

$c_1\ c_2\ c_3\ c_4$

$$H_{1,7} = \begin{matrix} c_1 \\ c_2 \\ c_3 \\ c_4 \end{matrix} \begin{bmatrix} 1 & 1 & 3 & 7 \\ 1 & 1 & 5 & 5 \\ 1/3 & 1/5 & 1 & 3 \\ 1/7 & 1/5 & 1/3 & 1 \end{bmatrix}$$

i. Average matrix for eighth consumer preference sub-factor: Problem-Solving

$c_1\ c_2\ c_3\ c_4$

$$H_{1,8} = \begin{matrix} c_1 \\ c_2 \\ c_3 \\ c_4 \end{matrix} \begin{bmatrix} 1 & 7 & 3 & 9 \\ 1/7 & 1 & 1/7 & 3 \\ 1/3 & 7 & 1 & 7 \\ 1/9 & 1/3 & 1/7 & 1 \end{bmatrix}$$

j. Average matrix for ninth consumer preference sub-factor: Entertainment

$c_1\ c_2\ c_3$

$$H_{1,9} = \begin{matrix} c_1 \\ c_2 \\ c_3 \end{matrix} \begin{bmatrix} 1 & 5 & 1 \\ 1/5 & 1 & 1/3 \\ 1 & 3 & 1 \end{bmatrix}$$

The *second expert group* was experts from academics and industry. Each "expert," where $p = 1, 2, 3, \ldots$, 16 individually carried out a pairwise evaluation by using Saaty's 1–9 scale (Chen, 2004; Saaty, 1980a, 1990, 2008b; Satty & Kearns, 1985) for the nine strategies and 32 sub-strategies adopted/implemented or thought to be important by organized retailers to address consumer preferences related to the organized retail environment.

The collected information was then summarized by calculating the average values of all 16 responses of experts (academic and industry experts) from the selected four cities in Odisha, and the final matrix obtained for further calculation/analysis is as follows:

a. Average matrix for retailers' nine principal counter-strategies

$$E_1 = \begin{array}{c} c_1 \\ c_2 \\ c_3 \\ c_4 \\ c_5 \\ c_6 \\ c_7 \\ c_8 \\ c_9 \end{array} \begin{array}{cccccccc} c_1 & c_2 & c_3 & c_4 & c_5 & c_6 & c_7 & c_8 & c_9 \end{array} \\ \left[\begin{array}{ccccccccc} 1 & 2 & 2 & 1/2 & 5 & 5 & 7 & 5 & 7 \\ 1/2 & 1 & 1/3 & 1/7 & 7 & 5 & 7 & 5 & 5 \\ 1/2 & 3 & 1 & 1/7 & 5 & 2 & 5 & 7 & 7 \\ 2 & 7 & 7 & 1 & 9 & 7 & 9 & 9 & 9 \\ 1/5 & 1/7 & 1/5 & 1/9 & 1 & 1/5 & 1/3 & 1/3 & 1 \\ 1/5 & 1/5 & 1/2 & 1/7 & 5 & 1 & 3 & 5 & 5 \\ 1/7 & 1/7 & 1/5 & 1/9 & 3 & 1/3 & 1 & 3 & 2 \\ 1/5 & 1/5 & 1/7 & 1/9 & 3 & 1/5 & 1/3 & 1 & 1 \\ 1/7 & 1/5 & 1/7 & 1/9 & 1 & 1/5 & 1/2 & 1 & 1 \end{array} \right]$$

Likewise, the pair-wise comparison (Saaty, 2008b) matrices for all 32 sub-strategies under nine principal strategies were prepared (as follows) for further analysis.

b. Average matrix for retailers' first counter sub-strategy: Store Atmosphere Rejuvenation

$c_1\ c_2\ c_3\ c_4$

$$E_{1.1} = \begin{array}{c} c_1 \\ c_2 \\ c_3 \\ c_4 \end{array} \left[\begin{array}{cccc} 1 & 3 & 3 & 1/3 \\ 1/3 & 1 & 1 & 1/3 \\ 1/3 & 1 & 1 & 1/2 \\ 3 & 3 & 2 & 1 \end{array} \right]$$

c. Average matrix for retailers' second counter sub-strategy: Value-Augmented Pricing

$c_1\ c_2\ c_3\ c_4$

$$E_{1.2} = \begin{array}{c} c_1 \\ c_2 \\ c_3 \\ c_4 \end{array} \left[\begin{array}{cccc} 1 & 1/5 & 1 & 1/5 \\ 5 & 1 & 7 & 3 \\ 1 & 1/7 & 1 & 1/5 \\ 5 & 1/3 & 5 & 1 \end{array} \right]$$

d. Average matrix for retailers' third counter sub-strategy: Merchandize Management

$$E_{1,3} = \begin{matrix} c_1 \\ c_2 \\ c_3 \end{matrix} \begin{bmatrix} 1 & 3 & 1/3 \\ 1/3 & 1 & 1/5 \\ 3 & 5 & 1 \end{bmatrix}$$

$c_1\ c_2\ c_3$

e. Average matrix for retailers' fourth counter sub-strategy: Customer Experience Management

$c_1\ c_2\ c_3\ c_4$

$$E_{1,4} = \begin{matrix} c_1 \\ c_2 \\ c_3 \\ c_4 \end{matrix} \begin{bmatrix} 1 & 1/3 & 3 & 5 \\ 3 & 1 & 7 & 9 \\ 1/3 & 1/7 & 1 & 5 \\ 1/5 & 1/9 & 1/5 & 1 \end{bmatrix}$$

f. Average matrix for retailers' fifth counter sub-strategy: Ease of Accessibility

$c_1\ c_2\ c_3$

$$E_{1,5} = \begin{matrix} c_1 \\ c_2 \\ c_3 \end{matrix} \begin{bmatrix} 1 & 5 & 9 \\ 1/5 & 1 & 3 \\ 1/9 & 1/3 & 1 \end{bmatrix}$$

g. Average matrix for retailers' sixth counter sub-strategy: Quality Management Practices

$c_1\ c_2\ c_3$

$$E_{1,6} = \begin{matrix} c_1 \\ c_2 \\ c_3 \end{matrix} \begin{bmatrix} 1 & 1 & 3 \\ 1 & 1 & 7 \\ 1/3 & 1/7 & 1 \end{bmatrix}$$

h. Average matrix for retailers' seventh counter sub-strategy: Customer Interaction Augmentation

$c_1\ c_2\ c_3\ c_4$

$$E_{1,7} = \begin{matrix} c_1 \\ c_2 \\ c_3 \\ c_4 \end{matrix} \begin{bmatrix} 1 & 1/2 & 3 & 1/3 \\ 2 & 1 & 7 & 1 \\ 1/3 & 1/7 & 1 & 1/5 \\ 3 & 1 & 5 & 1 \end{bmatrix}$$

i. Average matrix for retailers' eighth counter sub-strategy: Grievance Handling & Management
$c_1\ c_2\ c_3\ c_4$

$$E_{1.8} = \begin{array}{c} c_1 \\ c_2 \\ c_3 \\ c_4 \end{array} \begin{bmatrix} 1 & 7 & 5 & 7 \\ 1/7 & 1 & 1/5 & 1 \\ 1/5 & 5 & 1 & 5 \\ 1/7 & 1 & 1/5 & 1 \end{bmatrix}$$

j. Average matrix for retailers' ninth counter sub-strategy: Event Planning & Management
$c_1\ c_2\ c_3$

$$H_{19} = \begin{array}{c} c_1 \\ c_2 \\ c_3 \end{array} \begin{bmatrix} 1 & 3 & 5 \\ 1/3 & 1 & 3 \\ 1/5 & 1/3 & 1 \end{bmatrix}$$

Having prepared the average matrices for both the survey data, the next step was to calculate each decision criterion's preference level or weight score, rendering the overall goals' contribution. Every column was totaled after the pair-wise comparison matrix (A) for the criteria was set up in both cases. Every matrix element was separated by the sum of the column and normalized matrices for each criterion. Sub-criteria for both cases were set up (Eroglu, 2013). The sum of the entries in each column is 1 (Saaty, 2000). Finally, the priority vectors were established by computing the row averages of the normalized matrix for both cases. Prioritization meant the relative importance of a criterion about other criteria placed above it in the hierarchy. By computing the row means of the values in the normalized matrix (synthesis matrix) (N), general weight scores of the main criteria (key factors) were calculated using MS Excel 2007.

Likewise, the entire procedure was followed for all sub-criteria sets in both cases, i.e., the consumer and the retailer perspectives.

Based on the critical decision, a consistency check is an accepted way to examine the stability of the decision-maker's judgment in providing their judgments to the comparison matrix. However, it is tough to achieve the right consistency. Analytic Hierarchy Process (AHP) is helpful to determine the judgments provided in each hierarchy. An inconsistency ratio of less than or equal to 10% is usually satisfactory; in a few exclusive cases, higher values may be permitted (Saaty, 1990).

W (weighted sum vector), CI (consistency index), CR (consistency ratio), and RI (ratio index) are used for checking the consistency.

W is determined from the following equation:

$$Aw = \lambda_{max}$$

A is an observed matrix of pair-wise comparison, λ_{max} is a principal eigenvalue of A; w is the right eigenvector. The λ_{max} value is a vital validating parameter in AHP. It is used as the reference to screen information by computing the consistency ratio CR of the predicted vector to validate whether the pair-wise comparison matrix provides an entirely consistent evaluation. The consistency ratio (Saaty, 1990) is computed following the procedure illustrated in the mathematical formulation section of the chapter.

(i) Calculate the eigenvector or the relative weights and λ_{max} for each matrix of order n
(ii) Compute the consistency index for each matrix of order n by the formula:

$$CI = (\lambda_{max} - n)/(n - 1) \Rightarrow w = (w_1, w_2, ..., w_n)$$

(iii) The consistency ratio is then calculated using the formula:

$$CR = CI/RI$$

RI is the known random consistency index obtained from many simulations and diverges depending upon the order of the matrices. In the equation above, the closer the λ_{max} is to n, the higher the consistent detected values of A, so the difference between λ_{max} and n is a measure of consistency (Saaty & Vargas, 2012). Table 5.3 depicts the value of the random consistency index (RCI) for matrices of order 1–10 obtained by approximating random indices using a sample size of 500 (Saaty & Vargas, 2012).

According to Chang et al. (2007), the estimate is accepted If $CR \leq 0.1$; or, a new comparison matrix is considered until $CR \leq 0.1$. Saaty (2001) and Cheng and Li (2001) claim that the acceptable range differs according to the size of the matrix, i.e., 1.11 for a 5 by 5 matrix, 1.41 for an 8 by 8 matrix, and 0.1 for all bigger matrices. Suppose the value of CR is equivalent to or lesser than that value. In that case, it suggests that the computation within the matrix is adequate or indicates a better level of consistency in the comparative judgments, which are represented respectively in that matrix. On the other hand, if the CR value is higher than the acceptable value, its meaning is that the difference of judgments inside that matrix has taken place, and the evaluation process must hence be rechecked and modified. Usually, a CR value of 10% or less is acceptable (Saaty, 1980a). However, according to Saaty (2008b) and Saaty and Vargas (2012), any CR value greater than 10% is unacceptable. The judgments in the A matrix table should be reassessed to resolve discrepancy judgments provided in pair-wise comparison. An estimate of the eigenvalue can be evaluated by multiplying the whole of each column in a judgment matrix by its corresponding vector of weights.

For empirical analysis of both cases, the entire process (discussed in this chapter) is summarized in Table 5.10. The entire procedure for AHP is segregated into two phases. The first one is calculating the priority vector and priority ranking, and the second phase is the consistency check of the priority rankings.

The empirical analysis for both cases (consumer and retailers' perspectives) was performed separately using MS Excel following the rules summarized in Table 5.10.

Analysis of Local and Global Weight of Consumer Preferences (Consumer Perspective)

For prioritizing the factors for consumer preferences (consumer perspective), the average matrix obtained after calculating the geometric mean of 27 collected pair-wise matrices for consumer-preferred factors was further analyzed following the steps illustrated in Table 5.10. In the first phase, the column total was computed for each column. The normalized matrix was formulated by dividing each column element with the column total as the first step calculation. In the second step, the priority vector (PV) was calculated by summing up the row values for each factor, and the rank was assigned accordingly, which indicates the priority factors. The normalized (synthesis) matrix for the consumers' nine preferred factors with their priority vector and ranking are depicted in Tables 5.11 and 5.12.

Table 5.10 Steps for estimation procedure of AHP, *i*AHP and consistency check

Phase 1		Phase 2	
Calculation of Priority Vector (PV) & ranking		*Checking of consistency of PV*	
Step I	Calculation of column total in the average matrix	Step I	Calculation of Weighted Vector WV = (Average Matrix × PV)
	Formulation of Normalized (Synthesis) Matrix by dividing each column elements with respective column total	Step II	Calculation of Eigenvalues (λ = WV/PV)
Step II	Calculation of PV (Row averages)		Calculation of λ_{max} (i.e., an average of eigenvalues)
	Assigning ranks (Prioritization)	Step III	Calculation of CI = $(\lambda_{max} - n)/(n - 1)$
		Step IV	Checking RI from the table value
		Step V	Calculation of CR = CI/RI
			Consistency check CR < 0.10

The empirical analysis for both the cases (consumer perspective and retailers' perspective) was performed separately using MS Excel following the rules summarized in Table 6.10

Table 5.11 Calculation of normalized matrix for AHP (Consumer Perspective)

Factors	SA	PV	AST	ISD	CNV	PSQR	PPE	PS	ENT	Priority vector	Rank
Store atmosphere (SA)	0.0582	0.1190	0.0467	0.0373	0.1250	0.1122	0.1579	0.0580	0.0493	0.0849	4
Pricing and value (PV)	0.1165	0.2381	0.2336	0.2667	0.1750	0.2619	0.2030	0.2609	0.2463	0.2224	2
Assortment (AST)	0.2912	0.2381	0.2336	0.2667	0.1750	0.1122	0.1579	0.2029	0.1478	0.2028	3
In-store delight (ISD)	0.4077	0.2381	0.2336	0.2667	0.2250	0.3367	0.1579	0.2029	0.4433	0.2791	1
Convenience (CNV)	0.0116	0.0333	0.0327	0.0293	0.0250	0.0075	0.0226	0.0145	0.0163	0.0214	9
Product/service quality reliability (PSQR)	0.0192	0.0333	0.0771	0.0293	0.1250	0.0374	0.1128	0.0870	0.0163	0.0597	6
Person-to-person experience (PPE)	0.0082	0.0262	0.0327	0.0373	0.0250	0.0075	0.0226	0.0870	0.0069	0.0281	7
Problem-solving (PS)	0.0291	0.0262	0.0327	0.0373	0.0500	0.0123	0.0074	0.0290	0.0246	0.0276	8
Entertainment (ENT)	0.0582	0.0476	0.0771	0.0293	0.0750	0.1122	0.1579	0.0580	0.0493	0.0739	5

Source Estimated from Primary Data

After formulation of the normalized matrix, the next tasks were to check the priority vector's consistency as per the steps mentioned in Phase 2 in Table 5.11. In the first step of consistency check (Phase 2), the weighted vector (WV) was computed by multiplying the original average matrix with the priority vector (see Table 5.13)

Table 5.12 Calculation of Weighted Vector (WV) Matrix (Consumer Perspective)

Factors	SA	PV	AST	ISD	CNV	PSQR	PPE	PS	ENT	Priority vector	Weighted vector
Store atmosphere (SA)	1	0.5	0.2	0.14	5	3	7	2	1	0.0849	0.8881
Pricing and value (PV)	2	1	1	1	7	7	9	9	5	0.2224	2.3133
Assortment (AST)	5	1	1	1	7	3	7	7	3	0.2028	2.0698
In-store delight (ISD)	7	1	1	1	9	9	7	7	9	0.2791	3.0837
Convenience (CNV)	0.2	0.14	0.14	0.11	1	0.2	1	0.5	0.33	0.0214	0.2069
Product/service quality reliability (PSQR)	0.33	0.14	0.33	0.11	5	1	5	3	0.33	0.0597	0.5716
Person-to-person experience (PPE)	0.14	0.11	0.14	0.14	1	0.2	1	3	0.14	0.0281	0.2586
Problem-solving (PS)	0.5	0.11	0.14	0.14	2	0.33	0.33	1	0.5	0.0276	0.2708
Entertainment (ENT)	1	0.2	0.33	0.11	3	3	7	2	1	0.0739	0.7965

Source Estimated from Primary Data

Table 5.13 Calculation of eigen value (consumer perspective)

Factors	Priority vector (PV)	Weighted vector (WV)	Eigen value (λ)
Store atmosphere (SA)	0.0849	0.8881	10.466
Pricing and value (PV)	0.2224	2.3133	10.400
Assortment (AST)	0.2028	2.0698	10.205
In-store delight (ISD)	0.2791	3.0837	11.049
Convenience (CNV)	0.0214	0.2069	9.658
Product/service quality reliability (PSQR)	0.0597	0.5716	9.573
Person-to-person experience (PPE)	0.0281	0.2586	9.189
Problem-solving (PS)	0.0276	0.2708	9.796
Entertainment (ENT)	0.0739	0.7965	10.785

Source Estimated from Primary Data

Then in the next step, the eigenvalue $\lambda = WV/PV$ was calculated, and computing the average λ (see Table 5.13).

The third step, consistency index (CI), is to calculate the λ_{max} average λ. λ_{max} = Average of λi. In this case, $\lambda_{max} = 10.124$.

For checking the consistency ratio (CR), the consistency index was calculated as follows;

$$CR = CI/RI$$

$$CI = (\lambda_{max} - n)/(n - 1) = (10.124 - 9)/(9 - 1) = 0.14055627$$

For Random Index (RI), the Saaty Random Index table (see Table 5.3) was followed.

$$RI = (\text{for } n = 9) = 1.45$$

Therefore, CR = 0.14055627/1.45 = 0.0969 (CR $\leq$ 0.10)

Hence, the above-calculated priority weights are consistent, and the validated priority ranks of nine factors are shown in Table 5.14.

Similarly, the priority vectors and consistency of weights for all 32 sub-factors of nine consumer preference factors were calculated based on the above procedure. The local and global weights of nine-factor categories and 32 sub-factors for consumer preference in organized retailing are normalized based on the AHP analysis. The ranking for

Table 5.14 Priority ranks of consumers' preferred factors

Factors	Priority vector	Rank
Store atmosphere (SA)	0.0849	4
Pricing and value (PV)	0.2224	2
Assortment (AST)	0.2028	3
In-store delight (ISD)	0.2791	1
Convenience (CNV)	0.0214	9
Product/service quality reliability (PSQR)	0.0597	6
Person-to-person experience (PPE)	0.0281	7
Problem-solving (PS)	0.0276	8
Entertainment (ENT)	0.0739	5

Source Estimated from Primary Data

both local and global weights are shown in Table 5.15 and Fig. 5.4. For the goal of prioritization of consumer preferences, in level 2 of the hierarchy dealing with consumer preference factors, the evaluators considered *In-store Delights* (0.2791) as the most important criteria, followed by *Pricing & Value* (0.2224), *Assortment* (0.2028), *Store Atmospherics* (0.0849), *Entertainment* (0.0739), *Product/Service Quality & Reliability* (0.0597), *Person-to-Person Experience* (0.0281), *Problem-Solving* (0.0276), and *Convenience* (0.0214). As these nine-factor categories formed the second level of the goal, the local and the global weights are the same.

The visualization of priority weights (both local and global) is depicted in the decision tree structure shown in Fig. 5.4.

The local and global weights results are reported separately regarding the 32 consumer preference variables (in level 3 of the hierarchy structure). As far as the third hierarchy level, which consists of the sub-factors (variables), the top five most preferred sub-factors as per the global weight are—the latest and trendy products (0.0774) followed by prompt handling of customer complaints and queries (0.0622), value for money (0.0608), store facilities (0.0584) and fast and easy billing/POS and checkout (0.0578).

The bottom five consumer preference attributes (as per global weight) are found to be—guarantee/warranty (0.0048) at the bottom, followed by individual customer attention (0.0066), availability/never stockout (0.0071), affordability (0.0075), and location [prime market area] (0.0078) as listed in Table 5.16.

Table 5.15 Local and global weights of consumer preference factors and sub-factors

Sl. No.	Factor	Weight	Rank	Consistency indices	Sub-factors	Local weight (W)	Local rank	Consistency indices	Global weight (W/9)	Global rank
1	Store atmospherics	0.0849	4	Lambda Max = 10.124, N = 9, CI = 0.140, RI = 1.45, CR = 0.096; (CR < 0.10)	Ambiance	0.3001	2	Lambda Max = 4.096, N = 4, CI = 0.0320, RI = 0.9, CR = 0.0355	0.0333	15
					Aesthetic	0.1025	3		0.0114	24
					Cleanliness	0.0714	4		0.0079	27
					Store facilities	0.5258	1		0.0584	4
2	Pricing & value	0.2224	2		Value for money	0.5468	1	Lambda Max = 4.0816, N = 4, CI = 0.0272, RI = 0.9, CR = 0.0302	0.0608	3
					Discount and offers	0.1725	3		0.0192	19
					Affordability	0.0671	4		0.0075	29

(continued)

Table 5.15 (continued)

Sl. No.	Factor	Weight	Rank	Consistency indices	Sub-factors	Local weight (W)	Local rank	Consistency indices	Global weight (W/9)	Global rank
3	Assortment	0.2028	3		Loyalty rewards as cash discount/special offers	0.2133	2		0.0237	18
					Availability/never stock-out	0.0636	3	Lambda Max = 3.0224, N = 3, CI = 0.0112, RI = 0.58, CR = 0.0193	0.0071	30
					Latest and trendy products	0.6696	1		0.0744	1
					Attractive display/placement	0.2669	2		0.0297	16

Sl. No.	Factor	Weight	Rank	Consistency indices	Sub-factors	Local weight (W)	Local rank	Consistency indices	Global weight (W/9)	Global rank
4	In-store delights	0.2791	1		Touch & feel/in-store trail	0.2134	2	Lambda Max = 4.0878, N = 4, CI = 0.0293, RI = 0.9, CR = 0.0325	0.0237	17
					Fast & easy billing/POS & checkout	0.5206	1		0.0578	5
					In-store digitization	0.1223	4		0.0136	22
					Customer consultancy	0.1437	3		0.0160	20
5	Convenience	0.0214	9		One stop shopping	0.5095	1	Lambda Max = 3.0359, N = 3, CI = 0.0179, RI = 0.58, CR = 0.0309	0.0566	6

(continued)

Table 5.15 (continued)

Sl. No.	Factor	Weight	Rank	Consistency indices	Sub-factors	Local weight (W)	Local rank	Consistency indices	Global weight (W/9)	Global rank
6	Product/service quality & reliability	0.0597	6		Large/spacious store with proper layout & signage	0.4206	2		0.0467	10
					Location (prime market area)	0.0699	3		0.0078	28
					High-quality branded products	0.4868	1	Lambda Max = 3.0066, N = 3, CI = 0.0033, RI = 0.58, CR = 0.0057	0.0541	7
					Reliable & high-quality service (S)	0.4355	2		0.0484	9
					Reliable information sharing (about latest offerings)	0.0778	3		0.0086	26

Sl. No.	Factor	Weight	Rank	Consistency indices	Sub-factors	Local weight (W)	Local rank	Consistency indices	Global weight (W/9)	Global rank
7	Person-to-person experience	0.0281	7		Highly responsive/ prompt service	0.3951	2	Lambda Max = 4.0957, N = 4, CI = 0.0319, RI = 0.9, CR = 0.0354	0.0439	13
					Empathy/ politeness in employees' behavior	0.4175	1		0.0464	11
					Highly informative with good knowledge of offerings	0.1279	3		0.0142	21
					Individual customer attention	0.0595	4		0.0066	31

(continued)

Table 5.15 (continued)

Sl. No.	Factor	Weight	Rank	Consistency indices	Sub-factors	Local weight (W)	Local rank	Consistency indices	Global weight (W/9)	Global rank
8	Problem-solving	0.0276	8		Prompt handling of customer complaint & queries	0.5601	1	Lambda Max = 4.2346, N = 4, CI = 0.0782, RI = 0.9, CR = 0.0869	0.0622	2
					Listening to VOC/suggestions/feedback	0.0841	3		0.0093	25
					Hassle free exchange/return policy	0.3123	2		0.0347	14
					Guarantee/warranty	0.0435	4		0.0048	32

Sl. No.	Factor	Weight	Rank	Consistency indices	Sub-factors	Local weight (W)	Local rank	Consistency indices	Global weight (W/9)	Global rank
9	Entertainment	0.0739	5		Recreation/hangout	0.4798	1	Lambda Max = 3.0251, N = 3, CI = 0.0125, RI = 0.58, CR = 0.0216	0.0533	8
					Food zone	0.1146	3		0.0127	23
					Movies/shows or events	0.4057	2		0.0451	12
Total						9.00			1.00	

Source Estimated from Primary Data
The visualization of priority weights (both local and global) is depicted in the decision tree structure shown in Fig. 5.4

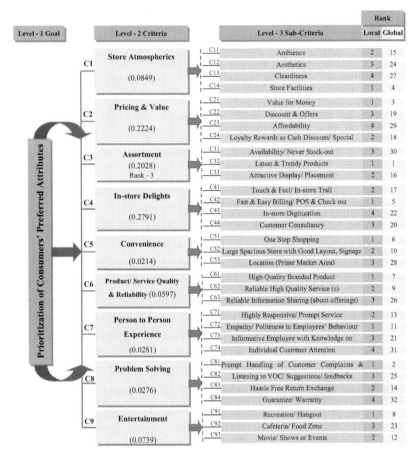

Fig. 5.4 Visualization of local and global weights of consumer preference

As per the local weight of consumer-preferred sub-factors is concerned, the sub-factor differentiated store facilities with the local weight of 0.5258 are found to be of top priority for consumers relative to the core factor store atmospherics, likewise value for money (0.5468) for pricing and value, latest and trendy products (0.6696) for assortment, easy billing/POS and checkout (0.5206) for in-store delights, one-stop shopping (0.5095) for convenience, high-quality branded products (0.4868) for the case of product/service quality and reliability, empathy and politeness

Table 5.16 Top and bottom five sub-factors of consumer preference

Sub-factors—consumers' perspective	
Consumers' top five priorities[a]	Consumers' bottom five priorities[a]
• Latest & trendy products • Prompt handling of customer complaints & queries • Value for money • Store facilities • Fast & easy billing/POS and checkout	• Guarantee/warranty • Individual customer attention • Availability/never stock-out • Affordability • Location (Prime Market Area)

[a] Based on Global Ranking in AHP

in employee behavior (0.4175) for a person-to-person experience, prompt handling of customer complaints and queries (0.5601) for problem-solving and recreation and hangout (0.4798) for the principal consumer preference factor of entertainment. However, global weight wise the top and bottom five sub-factors of consumer preference are depicted in Table 5.16.

In the retail business scenario, having identified and prioritized the consumer preferences only does not necessarily facilitate the retailers to address the consumers' priority preferences. Retailers must devise and implement relevant strategies to cater to consumer preferences and meet their expectations. As the consumers' preference set is vast and diverse, retailers must promptly explore enormous strategies to respond promptly to consumers' prioritized preferences. Further, retailers must ensure that they are offering the same what customers wish/expect to get. It is also necessary to examine if there is any difference in customers' preference priorities and the strategies retailers adopt on a priority basis to address customer preferences. Hence, to facilitate the large-format retailers to overcome such complications by endowing them with relevant, prioritized strategies and inputs, the second phase of AHP was carried out. In the second phase of AHP (as mentioned earlier), the consumers' preferred factors and sub-factors were interpreted through rigorous and meticulous expert mining. Hence, it is instead logically named *i*AHP, which is discussed in detail in the following section.

Analysis of Local and Global Weight of Retailers' Counter-Strategies (Retailer Perspective)

For prioritization of the factors for retailers' counter-strategies (retailer perspective), the average matrix obtained after calculation of the geometric mean of 16 collected pair-wise matrixes for retailers' strategies was further analyzed following the steps illustrated in Table 5.10, and the calculations were done likewise as performed for consumers' preference prioritization in the previous section. However, the entire procedure is repeated in this section (iAHP) also to avoid confusion. In the first phase, the column total was computed for each column. The normalized matrix was formulated by dividing each column element with the column total as the first step calculation. In the second step, the priority vector (PV) was calculated by summing up the row values for each factor, and the rank was assigned accordingly, which indicates the priority factors. Using the same procedure as above, the normalized (synthesis) matrix for the consumers' preferred nine factors with their priority vector and ranking are depicted in Table 5.17. The visualization of priority weights (both local and global) of retailers' counter-strategies and sub-strategies is depicted in the decision tree structure shown in Fig. 5.5.

Regarding the 32 sub-strategies (in level 3 of the hierarchy structure) adopted by retailers or thought to be important by retailers (as considered by experts), the local and global weight results are reported separately. As far as the third hierarchy level, which consists of the sub-strategies (variables) for this iAHP analysis, the top five most considered sub-strategies of retailers as per the global weight are—everything under one roof (0.0832) followed by visual merchandizing (0.0704), consumer socialization (0.0704), social response strategy (0.0682), and convenient billing/POS and checkout (0.0658). The bottom five sub-strategies, i.e., the sub-strategies for which retailers pay very negligible importance (as per global weight), are found to be—dedicated customer consultancy (0.0050) at the bottom, followed by employee orientation and knowledge up-gradation (0.0069), customer assurance building (0.0075), VOC management through community development (0.0075), and location planning and management (0.0079) as listed in Table 5.18.

As per the local weight of the sub-strategies is concerned, the sub-strategy differentiated store facilities with a local weight of 0.4419 are found to be of top priority for retailers for the principal strategy store atmosphere rejuvenation, likewise shopping hour-specific discounts

Table 5.17 Local and global weights of retailers' counter-strategy and sub-strategies

Sl. No.	Strategy	Weight	Rank	Consistency indices	Sub-strategy	Local weight (W)	Local rank	Consistency indices	Global weight (W/9)	Global rank
1	Store environment rejuvenation	0.1816	2	Lambda Max = 10.142, N = 9, CI = 0.14270872, RI = 1.45, CR = 0.0984 (CR < 0.1)	Architecture revival	0.2927	2	Lambda Max = 4.2269, N = 4, CI = 0.0756, RI = 0.9, CR = 0.084 (CR < 0.1)	0.0325	13
					Interior design	0.1229	4		0.0137	22
					Swachh drives (littering free environment)	0.1425	3		0.0158	20
					Differentiated store facilities	0.4419	1		0.0491	8
2	Value augmented pricing	0.129	4		Value based retailing	0.0800	3	Lambda Max = 4.1144, N = 4, CI = 0.0381, RI = 0.9, CR = 0.042 (CR < 0.1)	0.0089	26
					Shopping hour-specific discount and offers	0.5493	1		0.0610	6
					Reasonable pricing	0.0710	4		0.0079	27
					Direct cash discount	0.2997	2		0.0333	12

(continued)

Table 5.17 (continued)

Sl. No.	Strategy	Weight	Rank	Consistency indices	Sub-strategy	Local weight (W)	Local rank	Consistency indices	Global weight (W/9)	Global rank
3	Merchandise management	0.1351	3		Inventory/stock optimization	0.2600	2	Lambda Max = 3.0332, N = 3, CI = 0.0166, RI = 0.58, CR = 0.0286 (CR < 0.1)	0.0289	14
					Latest trend analytics & management	0.1060	3		0.0118	23
					Visual merchandising	0.6340	1		0.0704	2
4	Customer experience management	0.363	1		Dedicated product experience zone/facilities	0.2369	2	Lambda Max = 4.2170, N = 4, CI = 0.0723, RI = 0.9, CR = 0.080 (CR < 0.1)	0.0263	17
					Convenient billing/POS & checkout	0.5925	1		0.0658	5
					Digital information sharing & experience	0.1252	3		0.0139	21
					Dedicated customer consultancy	0.0454	4		0.0050	32

Sl. No.	Strategy	Weight	Rank	Consistency indices	Sub-strategy	Local weight (W)	Local rank	Consistency indices	Global weight (W/9)	Global rank
5	Ease of accessibility	0.0217	9		Everything under one roof	0.7485	1	Lambda Max = 3.0224, $N = 3$, CI = 0.0112, RI = 0.58, CR = 0.0193 (CR < 0.1)	0.0832	1
					Space planning & management	0.1805	2		0.0201	18
					Location planning & management	0.0710	3		0.0079	28
6	Quality management practices	0.0771	5		Product quality & brand management	0.3897	2	Lambda Max = 3.0713, $N = 3$, CI = 0.0356, RI = 0.58, CR = 0.0615 (CR < 0.1)	0.0433	10
					Service quality enhancement	0.5109	1		0.0568	7
					Trustworthy communication	0.0993	3		0.0110	25
7	Customer interaction augmentation	0.0401	6		Response time minimization	0.1663	3	Lambda Max = 4.0320, $N = 4$, CI = 0.0107, RI = 0.9, CR = 0.0118 (CR < 0.1)	0.0185	19

(continued)

Table 5.17 (continued)

Sl. No.	Strategy	Weight	Rank	Consistency indices	Sub-strategy	Local weight (W)	Local rank	Consistency indices	Global weight (W/9)	Global rank
					Employee grooming & behavioral excellence	0.3819	2		0.0424	11
					Employee orientation & knowledge up-gradation	0.0617	4		0.0069	31
					Customer touch-point attention	0.3901	1		0.0433	9
					Social response strategy	0.6142	1	Lambda Max = 4.1989, $N = 4$, CI = 0.0663, RI = 0.9, CR = 0.0737 (CR < 0.1)	0.0682	4
8	Grievance handling & management	0.0294	7		VOC management through community development	0.0672	3		0.0075	29
					No question (asked) exchange/return policy	0.2514	2		0.0279	16

Sl. No.	Strategy	Weight	Rank	Consistency indices	Sub-strategy	Local weight (W)	Local rank	Consistency indices	Global weight (W/9)	Global rank
9	Retail-tainment (Socialization)	0.0229	8		Customer assurance building	0.0672	4	Lambda Max = 3.0332, N = 3, CI = 0.0166, RI = 0.58, CR = 0.0286 (CR < 0.1)	0.0075	30
					Consumer socialization	0.6340	1		0.0704	3
					Cafeteria/food zone (development & promotion)	0.2600	2		0.0289	15
					Event-based crowd-sourcing	0.1060	3		0.0118	24
				Total		9.000			1.0000	

Source Estimated from Primary Data

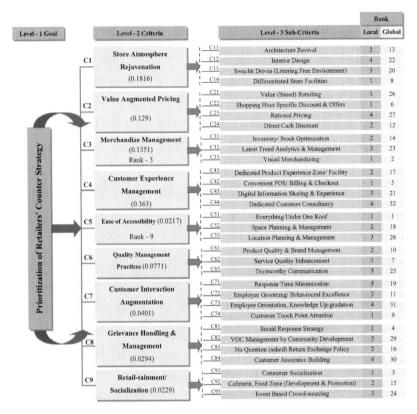

Fig. 5.5 Visualization of local and global weights of retailers' counter strategy & sub-strategies (*Source* Estimated from Primary Data)

and offers (0.5493) for value-augmented pricing, visual merchandizing (0.6340) for merchandise management, convenient billing/POS and checkout (0.5925) for customer experience management, everything under one roof (0.7485) for ease of accessibility, service quality enhancement (0.5109) for the case of quality management practices, customer touch-point attention (0.3901) for customer interaction augmentation, social response strategy (0.6142) for grievance handling and management and consumer socialization (0.6340) for the principal strategy of retailtainment/socialization.

Table 5.18 Top and bottom five sub-strategies of retailers' priority

Sub-strategies—retailers' perspective	
Retailers' top five priorities[a]	Retailers' bottom five priorities[a]
• Everything under one roof	• Dedicated customer consultancy
• Visual merchandizing	• Employee orientation & knowledge up-gradation
• Consumer socialization	• Customer assurance building
• Social response strategy	• VOC management through community development
• Convenient billing/POS and checkout	• Location planning & management

[a] Based on Global Ranking in AHP

IMPLICATIONS OF RESULTS (AHP FOR CONSUMERS' PERSPECTIVE VS. IAHP FOR RETAILERS' PERSPECTIVE)

This paper aimed to prioritize consumers' preferred factors and sub-factors and the strategies and sub-strategies used by organized large-format retailers to address consumer preferences. After ranking factors and sub-factors from a consumer perspective and strategies and sub-strategies from a retailer perspective based on priority vector (PV) and checking for consistency by calculating the consistency ratio (CR) and finding it to be valid in both cases, the researcher moved on to the primary purpose of the analysis, i.e., to determine whether there is any mismatch between customer and retailer expectations (as per ranks). To that end, the priorities from both the consumers' and retailers' perspectives are summarized in a matrix that depicts the match and mismatch in the consumers' preference hierarchy and retailers' offering (as shown in Table 5.19). As illustrated in the matrix (Table 5.19), there is a significant misalignment between the hierarchy in which consumers want their preferences addressed and the hierarchy in which organized retailers address those preferences. Only three consumer preference factors are addressed in the same order as the customers wish by retailers' relevant strategies. The other six consumer preference factors are addressed either ahead of time or with a delayed priority. In either case (earlier or later), retailers fail to develop a solution with the consumers' priority.

Table 5.19 The priority matrix: consumer vs. retailer perspective in organized retailing context

Consumers' Perspective	Retailers' Perspective	Remarks
In-Store Delights	Customer Experience Management	*Match*
Pricing & Value	Store Atmosphere Rejuvenation	Mismatch
Assortment	Merchandise Management	*Match*
Store Atmospherics	Value Augmented Pricing	Mismatch
Entertainment	Quality Management Practices	Mismatch
Product/Service Quality & Reliability	Customer Interaction Augmentation	Mismatch
Person to Person Experience	Grievance Handling & Management	Mismatch
Problem Solving	Retail-tainment/Socialization	Mismatch
Convenience	Ease of Accessibility	*Match*

Source Based on Primary Data Analysis

The matching color boxes represent consumer preferences and relevant retailer strategies. Where the color matches row-wise, the preference hierarchy of consumers and retailers coincides; otherwise, there is a mismatch in the priority of consumers' preferences and retailers' responses.

First and foremost, what consumers consider to be most important to them in organized retailing can also be used to tap the consumers' nerve and try to provide a better customer experience by implementing customer experience management strategies as their top priority. Customers' second most crucial preference is pricing and value, which means they want good value for their money. They expect reasonable and fair pricing. On the other hand, retailers put more effort into revitalizing their store atmosphere rather than considering value-augmented pricing strategy a secondary priority. In terms of importance, assortment falls to third place in the consumer's mind. The retailers simultaneously prioritize merchandise management as their third most crucial strategy, resulting in a perfect priority match. Store atmospherics are regarded as the fourth most crucial factor by organized retail shoppers. However, as a counter-strategy, store atmosphere rejuvenation is ranked second on the priority list of retailers. As such, it is a proactive response strategy used by retailers to attract customers. Customers rank entertainment as the fifth most important factor. The retailers, on the other hand, are not singing the same song. As a response strategy, retailtainment/socialization is ranked eighth on the retailers' priority list, resulting in a significant mismatch. Product/service quality and dependability are regarded as the sixth most important factor by organized retail shoppers. Retailers address this issue based on consumer priorities by implementing various quality management practices as their 5th priority. Person-to-person experience is the 7th most important factor in the consumers' priority list. This issue is also a spot ahead in the priority ladder of retailers and addressed beforehand. Organized retail shoppers think problem-solving is the 8th important factor; the relevant strategy adopted by retailers to address consumers' problems, i.e., grievance handling and management, can be spotted in the 7th spot on retailers' strategy priority list. The least preferred factor by consumers is convenience (in this study). To address this issue, retailers adopt the generic strategy of ease of accessibility, which is also at the bottom of the retailers' priority list. It is worth mentioning that addressing a factor or an issue of consumer preference beforehand is undoubtedly a reasonable effort, but addressing the other preferences gets disrupted in that race.

Hence, retailers must try to set the tune as per the string and address consumer preferences as per their priority, resulting in perfect harmony between customer and retailer. This is the true essence of a customer-centric retail culture. It is clear from the comparative analysis between consumer and retailer priorities that the priority hierarchy of "go-to market" strategies for retailers should be Customer Experience Management followed by Value-Augmented Pricing, Merchandise Management, Store Atmosphere Rejuvenation, Retail-tainment/Socialization, Quality Management Practices, Customer Interaction Augmentation, Grievance Handling & Management, and Layout & Location Planning.

Similarly, consumers' preferred sub-factors and retailers' counter-sub-strategies must be taken into account. The top five and bottom five criteria from the consumers' and retailers' perspectives were checked using global weights to investigate this issue.

Comparing the priority positions of those attributes and sub-strategies also resulted in a mismatch between consumers' priority regarding preference and retailers' priority in counter-strategy implementation to address those preferences. The comparative matrix prepared to examine this aspect is furnished in Table 5.20. If the comparative priority matrix (Table 5.20) will be observed concerning the identified consumers' preferred factors, sub-factors, and the retailer's counter-strategies, sub-strategies gleaned through interpretive expert mining (Tables 5.4 and 5.6 respectively), it can be found that consumers' preferences and retailers' adopted counter-strategies barely matches based on consumers' and retailers' priority. It merely indicates that organized retailers cannot address consumer preferences as per their priority. It depicts a clear picture that the organized retailer's focus is different from that of the consumers. However, it should also be remembered that the motive of consumers is different from that of retailers. Consumers are inevitably value seekers, whereas organized retailers possess a profit motive. Hence, it is pretty standard that their priorities shall also be different. In such a circumstance, the retailers must leverage their profit and customers' value, leading them to develop a customer-centric retail culture.

Table 5.20 Comparative analysis of consumers' vs. retailers' priorities (sub-criteria wise)

Priority	Consumer Perspective	Retailer Perspective	Remarks
Top 5 Priorities (Rank 1 to 5)	• Latest & Trendy Products	• Everything Under One Roof	Mismatch
	• Prompt Handling of Customer Complaints & Queries	• Visual Merchandizing	Mismatch
	• Value for Money	• Consumer Socialization	Mismatch
	• Store Facilities	• Social Response Strategy	Mismatch
	• Fast & Easy Billing/ POS and Checkout	• Convenient Billing/ POS and Checkout	**Match**
Bottom 5 Priorities (Rank 32 to 28)	• Guarantee/ Warranty	• Dedicated Customer Consultancy	Mismatch
	• Individual Customer Attention	• Employee Orientation & Knowledge Up-Gradation	Mismatch
	• Availability/ Never Stock-Out	• Customer Assurance Building	Mismatch
	• Affordability	• VOC Management through Community Development	Mismatch
	• Location [Prime Market Area]	• Location Planning & Management	**Match**

Source Based on estimated global ranks

Conclusion

This study prioritizes consumers' preferred factors, sub-factors, and retailers' counter-strategies and sub-strategies to see any misalignment. The prioritization process for this chapter began with the extraction and validation of consumer preference factors and sub-factors. The strategies and sub-strategies were first explored through interpretive expert mining to prioritize strategy and sub-strategies from the retailers' perspective. Both cases were examined, and it was discovered that there is a significant mismatch between the order of consumers' preferences and how retailers attempt to address those preferences. This mismatch is a significant impediment to a customer-centric, organized retail culture. As a result, to develop, adopt, and practice a customer-centric culture in organized retailing, retailers must leverage their strategic priorities according to the consumers' preferential priority ladder and offer strategies that provide unique customer benefits in an ever-changing retail environment. This chapter explores and illustrates what customers want and the order of their desires in terms of preferences, which can be referred to by existing as well as prospective large-format retailers to arm themselves with efficient strategic solutions in a proper hierarchy to match the customers' priorities and delight them in turn. The concluding chapter summarizes the entire study by addressing the "Objective" by providing a roadmap of customer-centric retailing with empirical support for organized retailers, which they can adopt and implement to practice a customer-centric retail culture. The recent economic downturn and uneven recovery have heightened the need to respond to change much more quickly and dramatically than ever before. In such volatile market conditions, organized retailers must understand subtle shifts in competitor movements and new consumer behavior and preferences to adopt a business model. They must acclimate to the proposed path to customer-centric retailing and make critical improvements to their operating model through continuous monitoring. Customer-centric businesses will thrive in the end because they strive for a balance of equity and efficiency, ensuring that both buyers and sellers benefit from their transactions and relationships. We want to reiterate that retail entities that can gain a competitive advantage by adopting a Customer-Centric Business Model (CCBM) will be competitive today and will continue to win tomorrow.

Acknowledgements Manoj Kumar Dash and Manash Kumar Sahu collected the data for this study. The data collection was not funded.

REFERENCES

Ahsan, K., & Rahman, S. (2016). An investigation into critical service determinants of customer to business (C2B) type product returns in retail firms. *International Journal of Physical Distribution and Logistics Management,* 46(6/7), 606–633. https://doi.org/10.1108/IJPDLM-09-2015-0235

Akaka, M. A., & Alden, D. L. (2010). Global brand positioning and perceptions: International advertising and global consumer culture. *International Journal of Advertising,* 29(1), 37–56. https://doi.org/10.2501/S02650487 09201026

Al-Harbi, K. M. A. S. (2001). Application of the AHP in project management. *International Journal of Project Management,* 19(1), 19–27. https://doi.org/10.1016/S0263-7863(99)00038-1

Anderson, J. L., Jolly, L. D., & Fairhurst, A. E. (2007). Customer relationship management in retailing: A content analysis of retail trade journals. *Journal of Retailing and Consumer Services,* 14(6), 394–399. https://doi.org/10.1016/j.jretconser.2007.02.009

Bayazit, O., & Karpak, B. (2007). An analytical network process-based framework for successful Total Quality Management (TQM): An assessment of Turkish manufacturing industry readiness. *International Journal of Production Economics,* 105(1), 79–96. https://doi.org/10.1016/j.ijpe.2005.12.009

Belch, M. A., & Willis, L. A. (2002). Family decision at the turn of the century: Has the changing structure of households impacted the family decision-making process? *Journal of Consumer Behaviour,* 2(2), 111–124. https://doi.org/10.1002/cb.94

Berman, R., Carson, D., MacCarthy, D., Moore, R. D., & Roddenberry, G. (1995). *Star trek voyager.* Paramount Pictures.

Bhattacharyya, J., Balaji, M. S., & Jiang, Y. (2023). Causal complexity of sustainable consumption: Unveiling the equifinal causes of purchase intentions of plant-based meat alternatives. *Journal of Business Research,* 156, 113511. https://doi.org/10.1016/j.jbusres.2022.113511

Chan, F. T. S., & Chan, H. K. (2010). An AHP model for selection of suppliers in the fast changing fashion market. *International Journal of Advanced Manufacturing Technology,* 51(9–12), 1195–1207. https://doi.org/10.1007/s00 170-010-2683-6

Chang, C. W., Wu, C. R., Lin, C. T., & Lin, H. L. (2007). Evaluating digital video recorder systems using analytic hierarchy and analytic network processes.

Information Sciences, 177(16), 3383–3396. https://doi.org/10.1016/j.ins. 2007.02.010

Chebat, J. C., Michon, R., Haj-Salem, N., & Oliveira, S. (2014). The effects of mall renovation on shopping values, satisfaction and spending behaviour. *Journal of Retailing and Consumer Services, 21*(4), 610–618. https://doi.org/10.1016/j.jretconser.2014.04.010

Chen, H. (2004). *A research based on fuzzy AHP for multi-criteria supplier selection in supply chain* [Master's Thesis, University in Taipei].

Chen, S. J., & Hwang, C. L. (1992). *Fuzzy multiple attribute decision making: Methods and applications.* Springer-Verlag.

Chen, S., Hwang, C., & Hwang, F. P. (1992). *Fuzzy multiple attribute decision making.* Springer.

Cheng, E. W. L., & Li, H. (2001). Information priority-setting for better resource allocation using analytic hierarchy process (AHP). *Information Management and Computer Security, 9*(2), 61–70. https://doi.org/10.1108/09685220110388827

Chernev, A., Böckenholt, U., & Goodman, J. (2015). Choice overload: A conceptual review and meta-analysis. *Journal of Consumer Psychology, 25*(2), 333–358. https://doi.org/10.1016/j.jcps.2014.08.002

Dabholkar, P. A. (1995). *A contingency framework for predicting causality between customer satisfaction and service quality.* ACR North American Advances.

Darden, W. R., & Ashton, D. (1974). Psychographic profiles of patronage preference groups. *Journal of Retailing, 50*(4), 99–112.

Ehrenberg, A. S. C. (1988). Repeat buying: Facts, theory and applications. reprinted in *Journal of Empirical Generalisations in Marketing Science.* Edward Arnold (Griffin), 5(2000), 392–770. http://www.empgens.com

Engel, J. F., & Blackwell, R. D. (1982). *Consumer behaviour* (4th ed.). Dryden.

Engel, J. F., Blackwell, R. D., & Miniard, P. W. (1986). *Consumer behaviour* (5th ed.). Dryden.

Engel, J. F., Kollat, D. T., & Blackwell, R. D. (1968). *Journal of Consumer Behaviour.* Rinehart & Winston.

Eroglu, E. (2013). Factors affecting consumer preferences for retail industry and retailer selection using analytic hierarchy process. *KAU IIBF Dergisi, 4*(6), 43–57.

Fader, P. S. (2012). *Customer centricity, Wharton executive essentials* (2nd ed). Wharton Digital Press.

Festinger, L. (1957). A theory of cognitive dissonance. In H. J. Westing & G. Albaum (Eds.) (1975), *Modern marketing thought* (3rd ed). Peterson, and Company. Collier-Macmillan Publishers.

Finn, A., & Louviere, J. J. (1996). Shopping center image, consideration, and choice: Anchor store contribution. *Journal of Business Research, 35*(3), 241–251. https://doi.org/10.1016/0148-2963(95)00129-8

Fisher, M., Rajaram, K., & Raman, A. (2001). Optimizing inventory replenishment of retail fashion products. *Manufacturing and Service Operations Management, 3*(3), 230–241. https://doi.org/10.1287/msom.3.3.230.9889

Gilly, M. C., & Hansen, R. W. (1985). Consumer complaint handling as a strategic marketing tool. *Journal of Consumer Marketing, 2*(4), 5–16. https://doi.org/10.1108/eb008139

Grewal, D., Levy, M., & Kumar, V. (2009). Customer experience management in retailing: An organizing framework. *Journal of Retailing, 85*(1), 1–14. https://doi.org/10.1016/j.jretai.2009.01.001

Grewal, D., Roggeveen, A. L., Sisodia, R., & Nordfält, J. (2017). Enhancing customer engagement through consciousness. *Journal of Retailing, 93*(1), 55–64. https://doi.org/10.1016/j.jretai.2016.12.001

Gumus, A. T. (2009). Evaluation of hazardous waste transportation firms by using a two step fuzzy-AHP and TOPSIS methodology. *Expert Systems with Applications, 36*(2), 4067–4074. https://doi.org/10.1016/j.eswa.2008.03.013

Guo, X. (2013). Living in a global world: Influence of consumer global orientation on attitudes toward global brands from developed versus emerging countries. *Journal of International Marketing, 21*(1), 1–22. https://doi.org/10.1509/jim.12.0065

Hari, S. G., Ram, D., Ravindran, S., & Reji, K. G. (2009). Study on decision making styles of consumers in malls a study with reference to malls in Ernakulam in Kerala. *IMS Manthan, 4*(2), 103–109.

Ho, W., Dey, P. K., & Higson, H. E. (2006), Multiple criteria decision-making techniques in higher education. *International Journal of Educational Management, 20*(5), 319–337. https://doi.org/10.1108/09513540610676403

Hoffman, K. D., & Turley, L. W. (2002). Atmospherics, service encounters and consumer decision making: An integrattve perspective. *Journal of Marketing Theory and Practice, 10*(3), 33–47. https://doi.org/10.1080/10696679.2002.11501918

Hoffman, M., Richmond, J., Morrow, J., & Salomone, K. (2002). Investigating "sense of belonging" in first-year college students. *Journal of College Student Retention: Research, Theory and Practice, 4*(3), 227–256. https://doi.org/10.2190/DRYC-CXQ9-JQ8V-HT4V

Howard, J. A., & Sheth, J. N. (1969). *The theory of buyer behavior*. John Wiley & Sons.

Hwang, C. L., & Yoon, K. (1981). *Multiple attribute decision making: Methods and applications: A state-of-the-art survey*. Springer-Verlag.

Ives, B., Cossick, K., & Adams, D. (2019). Amazon Go: Disrupting retail? *Journal of Information Technology Teaching Cases, 9*(1), 2–12. https://doi.org/10.1177/2043886918819092

Jackson, J. (2001). Prioritising customers and other stakeholders using the AHP. *European Journal of Marketing, 35*(7/8), 858–873. https://doi.org/10.1108/EUM0000000005728

Jacoby, J., Chestnut, R. W., & Silberman, W. S. (1977). Consumer use and comprehension of nutrition information. *Journal of Consumer Research, 4*(2), 119–128. https://doi.org/10.1086/208687

Jha, N., & Mahmoud, A. (2017, February). Mining user requirements from application store reviews using frame semantics. In *International working conference on requirements engineering: Foundation for software quality* (pp. 273–287). Springer. https://doi.org/10.1007/978-3-319-54045-0_20

Jin, B., & Kim, J. O. (2003). A typology of Korean discount shoppers: Shopping motives, store attributes, and outcomes. *International Journal of Service Industry Management, 14*(4), 396–419. https://doi.org/10.1108/09564230310489240

Kamaladevi, B. (2010). Customer experience management in retailing. *Business Intelligence Journal, 3*(1), 37–54.

Khare, A. (2012). Impact of consumer decision–making styles on Indian consumers' mall shopping behaviour. *International Journal of Indian Culture and Business Management, 5*(3), 259–279. https://doi.org/10.1504/IJICBM.2012.046624

Kim, J. E., & Kim, J. H. (2016). Consumer socialization on adolescent impulsive buying behavior through school and parents: A random effects model. *Family and Environment Research, 54*(4), 385–395. https://doi.org/10.6115/fer.2016.029

Kohler, T., & Nickel, M. (2017). Crowdsourcing business models that last. *Journal of Business Strategy, 38*(2), 25–32. https://doi.org/10.1108/JBS-10-2016-0120

Krugman, H. E. (1965). The impact of television advertising: Learning without involvement. *Public Opinion Quarterly, 29*(3), 349–356. https://doi.org/10.1086/267335

Lal, R., & Matutes, C. (1994). Retail pricing and advertising strategies. *Journal of Business, 67*(3), 345–370. https://doi.org/10.1086/296637

Lastovicka, J. L. (1982). On the validation of lifestyle traits: A review and illustration. *Journal of Marketing Research, 19*(1), 126–138. https://doi.org/10.1177/002224378201900112

Lee, K., Joshi, K., & Bae, M. (2008). Using analytical hierarchy process (AHP) to identify the relative importance of the features needed for web-based systems development. *Information Resources Management Journal, 21*(3), 88–100. https://doi.org/10.4018/irmj.2008070105

Lindblom, A., Kajalo, S., & Mitronen, L. (2016). Does a retailer's charisma matter? A study of frontline employee perceptions of charisma in the retail setting. *Journal of Services Marketing, 30*(3), 266–276. https://doi.org/10.1108/JSM-05-2015-0160

Lysonski, S., & Durvasula, S. (2013). Consumer decision making styles in retailing: Evolution of mindsets and psychological impacts. *Journal of Consumer Marketing, 30*(1), 75–87. https://doi.org/10.1108/07363761311290858

Moschis, G. P. (1976). Shopping orientations and consumer uses of information. *Journal of Retailing, 52*(2), 61–70.

Motakiaee, R. (2011). *Multi Criteria Decision Making (MCDM) models in fuzzy and nonfuzzy environments.* SSRN 1761559

Mühlbacher, A. C., & Kaczynski, A. (2016). Making good decisions in healthcare with multi-criteria decision analysis: The use, current research and future development of MCDA. *Applied Health Economics and Health Policy, 14*(1), 29–40. https://doi.org/10.1007/s40258-015-0203-4

Newman, C. L., Howlett, E., Burton, S., Kozup, J. C., & Heintz Tangari, A. (2012). The influence of consumer concern about global climate change on framing effects for environmental sustainability messages. *International Journal of Advertising, 31*(3), 511–527. https://doi.org/10.2501/IJA-31-3-511-527

Nicosia, F. M. (1966). *Consumer decision processes; marketing and advertising implications.* Prentice Hall.

Nurhayati, T., & Hendar, H. (2017). Customer interaction management capabilities on the micro-retail fashion in Indonesia. *Journal of Relationship Marketing, 16*(1), 1–20.

Olshavsky, R. W., & Granbois, D. H. (1979, September 6). Consumer decision making-fact or fiction? *Journal of Consumer Research, 6*(2), 93–100. https://doi.org/10.1086/208753

Pachauri, M. (2001). Consumer behaviour: A literature review [Review]. *Marketing Review, 2*(3), 319–355. https://doi.org/10.1362/1469347012569896

Porter, S. S., & Claycomb, C. (1997). The influence of brand recognition on retail store image. *Journal of Product and Brand Management, 6*(6), 373–387. https://doi.org/10.1108/10610429710190414

Reed, K., Goolsby, J. R., & Johnston, M. K. (2016). Listening in and out: Listening to customers and employees to strengthen an integrated market-oriented system. *Journal of Business Research, 69*(9), 3591–3599. https://doi.org/10.1016/j.jbusres.2016.01.002

Saaty, T. L. (1978). Modeling unstructured decision problems — The theory of analytical hierarchies. *Mathematics and Computers in Simulation, 20*(3), 147–158. https://doi.org/10.1016/0378-4754(78)90064-2

Saaty, T. L. (1980a, November). *The analytic hierarchy process (AHP) for decision making.* http://www.cashflow88.com/decisiones/saaty1.pdf. In Kobe.

Saaty, T. L. (1980b). *The analytic hierarchy process*. McGraw-Hill.
Saaty, T. L. (1985). *Decision making for leaders*. Life Time Leaning Publications.
Saaty, T. L. (1990). How to make a decision: The analytic hierarchy process. *European Journal of Operational Research, 48*(1), 9–26. https://doi.org/10.1016/0377-2217(90)90057-I
Saaty, T. L. (2000). *Fundamentals of decision making and priority theory* (2nd ed.). RWS Publications.
Saaty, T. L. (2001). Fundamentals of the analytic hierarchy process. In D. L. Schmoldt, J. Kangas, G. A. Mendoza, & M. Pesonen (Eds.), *The analytic hierarchy process in natural resource and environmental decision making. Managing forest ecosystems* (Vol. 3, pp. 15–35). Springer. https://doi.org/10.1007/978-94-015-9799-9_2
Saaty, T. L. (2008a). Decision making with the analytic hierarchy process. *International Journal of Services Sciences, 1*(1), 83–98. https://doi.org/10.1504/IJSSCI.2008.017590
Saaty, T. L. (2008b). Relative measurement and its generalization in decision making why pairwise comparisons are central in mathematics for the measurement of intangible factors the analytic hierarchy/network process. *RACSAM-Revista de la Real Academia de Ciencias Exactas, Fisicas y Naturales. Serie A. Matematicas, 102*(2), 251–318. https://doi.org/10.1007/BF03191825
Saaty, T. L., & Kearns, K. P. (1991). *Analytical planning: The organization of systems* (Vol. 4). The Analytic Hierarchy Process Series. RWS Publications.
Saaty, T. L., & Vargas, L. G. (2012). The seven pillars of the analytic hierarchy process. In *Models, methods, concepts and applications of the analytic hierarchy process* (pp. 23–40). Springer. https://doi.org/10.1007/978-1-4614-3597-6_2
Satty, T. L., & Kearns, K. P. (1985). *Analytical planning: The organization of systems*. The Analytic Hierarchy Process Series, *4*.
Seiders, K., Berry, L. L., & Gresham, L. G. (2000). Attention, retailers! How convenient is your convenience strategy? *MIT Sloan Management Review, 41*(3), 79.
Shah, D., Rust, R. T., Parasuraman, A., Staelin, R., & Day, G. S. (2006). The path to customer centricity. *Journal of Service Research, 9*(2), 113–124. https://doi.org/10.1177/1094670506294666
Shang, G., Pekgün, P., Ferguson, M., & Galbreth, M. (2017). How much do online consumers really value free product returns? Evidence from EBay. *Journal of Operations Management, 53–56*(1), 45–62. https://doi.org/10.1016/j.jom.2017.07.001
Smith, S. A., & Agrawal, N. (2000). Management of multi-item retail inventory systems with demand substitution. *Operations Research, 48*(1), 50–64. https://doi.org/10.1287/opre.48.1.50.12443

Solomon, M. R. (1987). The role of the surrogate consumer in service delivery. *Service Industries Journal, 7*(3), 292–307. https://doi.org/10.1080/02642068700000034

Sproles, E. K., & Sproles, G. B. (1990). Consumer decision-making styles as a function of individual learning styles. *Journal of Consumer Affairs, 24*(1), 134–147. https://doi.org/10.1111/j.1745-6606.1990.tb00262.x

Sproles, G. B. (1985). From perfectionism to fadism: Measuring consumers' decision-making styles. In *Proceedings, American Council on Consumer Interests* (Vol. 31, No. 2, pp. 79–85). ACCI.

Sprotles, G. B., & Kendall, E. L. (1986). A methodology for profiling consumers' decision-making styles. *Journal of Consumer Affairs, 20*(2), 267–279. https://doi.org/10.1111/j.1745-6606.1986.tb00382.x

Srivastava, R. K. (2008). Changing retail scene in India. *International Journal of Retail and Distribution Management, 36*(9), 714–721. https://doi.org/10.1108/09590550810890957

Stein, A., & Ramaseshan, B. (2016). Towards the identification of customer experience touch point elements. *Journal of Retailing and Consumer Services, 30*, 8–19. https://doi.org/10.1016/j.jretconser.2015.12.001

Talib, F., Rahman, Z., & Qureshi, M. N. (2011). A study of total quality management and supply chain management practices. *International Journal of Productivity and Performance Management, 60*(3), 268–288. https://doi.org/10.1108/17410401111111998

Tsinidou, M., Gerogiannis, V., & Fitsilis, P. (2010). Evaluation of the factors that determine quality in higher education: An empirical study. *Quality Assurance in Education, 18*(3), 227–244. https://doi.org/10.1108/09684881011058669

Tzeng, G. H., & Huang, J. J. (2011). *Multiple attribute decision making: Methods and applications*. CRC Press.

Vaidya, O. S., & Kumar, S. (2006). Analytic hierarchy process: An overview of applications. *European Journal of Operational Research, 169*(1), 1–29. https://doi.org/10.1016/j.ejor.2004.04.028

Walsh, G., Hennig-Thurau, T., & Mitchell, V. W. (2007). Consumer confusion proneness: Scale development, validation, and application. *Journal of Marketing Management, 23*(7–8), 697–721. https://doi.org/10.1362/026725707X230009

Wang, Q., & Shukla, P. (2013). Linking sources of consumer confusion to decision satisfaction: The role of choice goals. *Psychology and Marketing, 30*(4), 295–304. https://doi.org/10.1002/mar.20606

Wanninayake, B. W. M. C. (2014). Consumer decision-making styles and local brand biasness: Exploration in the Czech Republic. *Journal of Competitiveness, 6*(1), 3–17. https://doi.org/10.7441/joc.2014.01.01

Ward, S. (1974). Consumer socialization. *Journal of Consumer Research*, *1*(2), 1–14. https://doi.org/10.1086/208584

Wells, W. D. (2011). *Life style and psychographics*. Marketing Classics Press.

Wesley, S., LeHew, M., & Woodside, A. G. (2006). Consumer decision-making styles and mall shopping behavior: Building theory using exploratory data analysis and the comparative method. *Journal of Business Research*, *59*(5), 535–548. https://doi.org/10.1016/j.jbusres.2006.01.005

White, D. G. (2010). *Sinister yogis*. University of Chicago Press.

Zamarrón-Mieza, I., Yepes, V., & Moreno-Jiménez, J. M. (2017). A systematic review of application of multi-criteria decision analysis for aging-dam management. *Journal of Cleaner Production*, *147*, 217–230. https://doi.org/10.1016/j.jclepro.2017.01.092

Recommended Readings

Baumgartner, H., & Homburg, C. (1996). Applications of structural equation modeling in marketing and consumer research: A review. *International Journal of Research in Marketing, 13*(2), 139–161. https://doi.org/10.1016/0167-8116(95)00038-0

Chin, W. W., Peterson, R. A., & Brown, S. P. (2008). Structural equation modeling in marketing: Some practical reminders. *Journal of Marketing Theory and Practice, 16*(4), 287–298. https://doi.org/10.2753/MTP1069-6679160402

Gupta, S., & Ramachandran, D. (2021). Emerging market retail: Transitioning from a product-centric to a customer-centric approach. *Journal of Retailing, 97*(4), 597–620. https://doi.org/10.1016/j.jretai.2021.01.008

Hair, J. F. (2009). *Multivariate data analysis*. Pearson.

Hair, J. F., Hult, G. T. M., Ringle, C. M., Sarstedt, M., & Thiele, K. O. (2017). Mirror, mirror on the wall: A comparative evaluation of composite-based structural equation modeling methods. *Journal of the Academy of Marketing Science, 45*(5), 616–632. https://doi.org/10.1007/s11747-017-0517-x

Hair, J. F., Ringle, C. M., & Sarstedt, M. (2012a). Partial least squares: The better approach to structural equation modeling? *Long Range Planning, 45*(5–6), 312–319. https://doi.org/10.1016/j.lrp.2012.09.011

Hair, J. F., Sarstedt, M., Ringle, C. M., & Mena, J. A. (2012b). An assessment of the use of partial least squares structural equation modeling in marketing research. *Journal of the Academy of Marketing Science, 40*(3), 414–433. https://doi.org/10.1007/s11747-011-0261-6

Steenkamp, J. E. M., & Baumgartner, H. (2000). On the use of structural equation models for marketing modeling. *International Journal of Research in Marketing, 17*(2–3), 195–202. https://doi.org/10.1016/S0167-8116(00)00016-1

Wind, Y., & Saaty, T. L. (1980). Marketing applications of the analytic hierarchy process. *Management Science, 26*(7), 641–658. https://doi.org/10.1287/mnsc.26.7.641

Index

A
Amazon, 20, 32
Analytical Hierarchal Approach, 91
Analytic Hierarchy Process (AHP), 92, 93, 98–104, 106, 109, 111, 120, 123–125, 127, 133–137, 139, 149, 157
average variance extracted (AVE), 63, 68–70, 72

B
Bartlett's test of sphericity, 50, 52, 57, 62
BPA, 17
brick-and-mortar store, 39

C
Complex Decision Making, 97
component matrix, 50
Confirmatory Factor Analysis (CFA), 47, 50, 51, 63, 72, 77, 84, 107, 127
consumer decision making style, 41, 93–97
consumer perspective, 93, 99, 110, 135–139, 157, 161
consumer preference, 5, 26, 40, 43, 44, 46, 50, 52, 53, 63, 72, 77, 79, 81, 83–86, 92, 93, 98, 100, 107–109, 111, 113, 120, 122, 127–130, 135, 139–141, 148, 149, 157, 159, 160, 162
Customer-Centered Behaviour (CCB), 42
customer-centric, 3–7, 10–12, 14–21, 31, 32, 34, 39–44, 86, 91, 92, 160, 162
Customer-Centric Business Model (CCBM), 43, 86, 91, 162
customer centricity, 3, 4, 9–18, 21, 32, 40, 41, 45, 46, 71, 83, 92, 93
customer-centric marketing, 9, 26, 41
customer-centric organization, 11, 16, 21

© The Editor(s) (if applicable) and The Author(s), under exclusive license to Springer Nature Singapore Pte Ltd. 2023
M. K. Dash et al., *Customer-Centricity in Organized Retailing*,
https://doi.org/10.1007/978-981-19-3593-0

customer experience, 12, 14, 20, 25, 42, 110, 112, 113, 156, 158, 159
Customer Experience Management, 116, 132, 152, 160
customer focus, 42
"Customer Lifetime Value (CLV)", 40, 92
customer relationship, 14, 15, 124
customer satisfaction, 20, 42, 43, 117
customer segmentation, 5
customer service, 16, 17, 20, 32, 42

D
Decision maker (DM), 97, 125, 133
direct marketing, 13

E
e-commerce, 14, 20
emerging markets (EMs), 4, 6, 25, 27–30, 33
empirical analysis, 40, 46, 52, 127, 135, 136
employment, 28
expert mining, 98, 100, 109, 113, 120, 124, 127, 149, 160, 162
Exploratory factor analysis (EFA), 47, 49, 50, 52, 63, 107, 127

F
Fader, Peter, 11, 17, 18, 92

G
global retail, 91
goodness-of-fit (GOF), 51, 70, 72, 77

H
heavy shoppers, 123, 124, 127

hedonic, 41, 43–46, 49, 51, 53, 79–81, 83–85
"*Hedonic Motive*", 59, 60, 68, 71, 77
hiring policy, 33

I
"Interpretive AHP (iAHP)", 98–100, 109, 111, 136, 149, 150, 157

K
Kaiser-Meyer-Olkin (KMO), 47, 50, 52, 57, 62

M
Multi-Criteria Decision Making (MCDM), 97, 98, 100, 102, 104
Multiple Attribute Decision Making (MADM), 97
Multiple Objective Decision Making (MODM), 97

O
Organized and Unorganized Retailers, 9
organized retail/organized retailing, 4–6, 25–31, 33, 34, 39–41, 43–46, 49, 51–53, 72, 79, 81, 83–86, 91–93, 98, 107, 109–111, 113, 117, 118, 122, 124, 127, 130, 139, 159, 162

P
Partial Least Squares (PLS), 75, 76
patronage intention, 5, 41, 43, 44, 46, 51–53, 59, 61, 62, 79, 80, 83
person to person experience (PPE), 58, 71, 77, 79, 81, 83, 84, 108,

110, 129, 137–140, 145, 149, 158
pricing and value, 53, 79, 113, 123, 137–140, 159
principal component analysis, 49, 52
Principal Component Factor Analysis (PCFA), 84
problem-solving, 77, 94, 95, 100, 110, 113, 123, 149, 159
product centricity, 14, 17

R
retailer perspective, 100, 114, 133, 150, 157, 158, 161
retail service quality (RSQS), 45
retailtainment/socialization, 120, 156, 159

S
service encounters, 96
service-focused culture, 21
service quality, 32, 45
service quality dimensions (SERVQUAL), 45
SERVPERF, 45
shopping motivation, 5, 40, 41, 43, 44, 46, 49, 50, 53, 59, 62, 72, 77, 79, 80, 83
SMPI Model, 40, 71, 78, 81
squared inner construct correlation (SIC), 70, 72

store atmospherics (SA), 46, 54, 71, 77, 79, 81, 83, 84, 108, 110, 113, 114, 128, 141, 148, 158, 159
structural equation model (SEM), 40, 51, 72, 77, 85, 86
supermarket/hypermarket, 44, 45, 49, 53, 58, 59, 79–81, 83, 85
supermarket retailers, 31, 43

T
Technopak, Microsoft Corp., PWC, Peper & Rogers, KPMG, ATKearney, Booz-Allen Hamilton, IBM Business Consultancy, 41

U
unorganized retailing, 26, 28, 29
utilitarian, 41, 43–46, 49, 51, 53, 79–81, 83–85
"*Utilitarian Motive*", 59, 60, 68, 71, 77

W
Wunderman, Lester, 13

Z
Zappos, 20, 21

Printed in the United States
by Baker & Taylor Publisher Services